SIDE DISH RECIPES

A One-of-a-kind Homemade Potato Side Dish Cookbook

(Happiness Is When You Have a Beginner Side Dish Cookbook!)

Elva Perez

Published by Alex Howard

© **Elva Perez**

All Rights Reserved

*Side Dish Recipes: A One-of-a-kind Homemade Potato Side Dish Cookbook
(Happiness Is When You Have a Beginner Side Dish Cookbook!)*

ISBN 978-1-990169-71-7

All rights reserved. No part of this guide may be reproduced in any form without permission in writing from the publisher except in the case of brief quotations embodied in critical articles or reviews.

Legal & Disclaimer

The information contained in this book is not designed to replace or take the place of any form of medicine or professional medical advice. The information in this book has been provided for educational and entertainment purposes only.

The information contained in this book has been compiled from sources deemed reliable, and it is accurate to the best of the Author's knowledge; however, the Author cannot guarantee its accuracy and validity and cannot be held liable for any errors or omissions. Changes are periodically made to this book. You must consult your doctor or get professional medical advice before using any of the suggested remedies, techniques, or information in this book.

Table of contents

Part 1 1
Introduction 2
Vegetarian Casserole Recipes 3
Butternut Squash Casserole 3
Eggplant Lasagna 5
Candied Sweet Potato Casserole 7
Summer Squash Casserole 9
Layered Cheesy Vegetable Casserole 11
Cheesy Potato & Zucchini Casserole 13
Pasta & White Bean Casserole 14
Spinach & Rice Casserole 16
Black Bean Casserole 18
Basil Tomato & Zucchini Casserole 20
Spinach, Potato & Mushrooms Casserole 22
Eggplant, Lentil & Cheese Casserole 24
Wild Rice Casserole 26
Baked Candied Yam & Apple Casserole 27
Vegetarian Mexican Casserole 29
Tortellini Zucchini Casserole 31
Tater Tot Casserole 32
Mexicaly's Corn And Red Bean Casserole 34
Vegetarians' White Beans And Spinach With Silk Tofu ... 36
Rainbow Veggie Dish 38
Cabbage, Lentil & Potato Casserole 40
Hot And Sweet Potatoes With Fried Tofu Squares 42

"Tres" (3) Mushroom Casserole 44
Stuffed Bell Peppers With Soy Sauce 46
Mediterranean Casserole 49
Spicy-Sweet Pumpkin And Eggplant Lasagne 51
Bread And Chickpeas Curry Casserole 53
Tofu Squares And Mushrooms With Angel's Pasta 55
Stuffed Lettuce Rolls With Nuts And Berries 58
Breadfruit And White Beans Casserole 60
Pumpkin-Parsnip With Apples Casserole 62
Lentil-Tomato Curry 64
Brown Rice With Veggie Casserole 66
Manila Red Beans And Rice Casserole 68
Couscous, Beans And Corn Burritos 70
Black Eyed Peas With Mushroom Casserole 72
5 S-T-A-R Veggie Casserole 74
Honey Sweet Potato's Stew 75
Sweet Hearty Fruit-Veggie Stew 77
Couscous And Veggie Burger Stew 79
Baked Potato Pockets With Nutty Pineapple Stew 82
Stuffed Eggplants With Apples Casserole 85
Stuffed Pumpkin With Chestnuts Casserole 88
Stuffed Beefsteak Tomatoes With Fruit Casserole 91
Any Holiday Veggie Casserole 94
Veggie Meat With Figs Casserole 96
Pesto Lasagna With Pine Nuts And Penne 98
Vietnamese Rolls With Special Vegan Sauce 101
Spicy Lettuce Rolls With Fruity Stew 104

Saba Burgers With Veggie Stew Sauce 107
5 Ingredients Or Less Vegetarian Recipes 109
Almond Broccoli Salad 109
Apple Celery Salad 110
Apple Pear Salad 111
Asian Lettuce Wraps 113
Avocado Dip 114
Baked Bean Soup 115
Baked Eggplant Sandwiches 117
Baked Mac And Cheese 119
Bean Burritos 120
Cranberry Crumble 121
Chorizo Beans 123
Easy Chimis 124
Easy Pot Pie 125
Famous Cabbage Soup 126
Garlic Brussels Sprouts 127
Green Bean And Lentil Stew 128
Grilled Cheese And Peppers On Sour Dough 130
Lemon Basil Pasta 132
Lentil Soup 133
Part 2 134
Introduction 135
Mcdonalds Fries 137
Mexican Style Corn 139
Microwave Cornonthecob In The Husk 141
Mouthwatering Brown Sugar Bacon 143

My Muminlaws Lightly Fried Plantains 144

Nancys Butter Beans 145

No Cook Applesauce 147

Nutmeg Mashed Potatoes 148

Orange Wild Rice With Pistachios And Cranberries 150

Oven Baked Parsley Red Potatoes 151

Oven Roasted Baked Potatoes 152

Ovenbaked Potato Fries 154

Ovenroasted Broccolini 155

Paleo Cauliflower Rice 156

Paleo Yam Dish 158

Panfried Asparagus With Onions 159

Panfried Fennel 160

Parmesanroasted Tomatoes 161

Patacones De Colombia Fried Plantains 163

Pinto Beans Muy Facil 164

Pomegranate Glazed Carrots 166

Quick And Easy Baked Carrots 168

Quick And Easy Grilled Potatoes 170

Quick And Easy Mashed Sweet Potatoes 171

Quick And Easy Panroasted Brussels Sprouts With Gorgonzola Cheese 173

Quick And Easy Parmesan Zucchini Fries 174

Quick And Spicy Spaghetti Squash 176

Quick Asparagus Stirfry 178

Quick Savory Grilled Peaches 180

Quick Zucchini Side Dish With Toasted Almonds 182

Raisin Plantains 183
Ramp Potatoes 185
Really Simple Rice 186
Roasted Asparagus With Herb Goat Cheese 187
Roasted Buffalo Brussels Sprouts 188
Roasted Butternut Squash Puree 189

Part 1

Introduction

This specific cookbook is all about serving meals. Inside you will find 200 various vegetarian recipes for your breakfast, brunch, lunch, dinner and snacks. These recipes are made specifically to make the recipe as casseroles, salads, side dishes or with only 5 ingredients or less.

There is a wide variety of vegetarian choices inside, I hope you find some great recipes within!

I hope you find some new recipes you want to try today!

Vegetarian Casserole Recipes

Butternut Squash Casserole

This excellent dish with a fusion of flavors is perfect for winter evenings.

Ingredients:

4 cups of butternut squash, peeled and cubed into ½-inch size
½ teaspoon of salt
½ teaspoon of black pepper
1 tablespoon of olive oil
`1/4 cup of cream cheese
1 cup of asiago cheese, divided
½ cup of parmesan cheese, divided
1 egg
1 cup of breadcrumbs, divided

Directions:

Preheat oven to 400 degrees F. Grease a baking dish. In a bowl, add butternut squash, salt, pepper and oil and toss well. Roast for 15 to 20 minutes or till tender.

Place roasted butternut squash in a large bowl. Reduce the temperature of oven to 350 degrees F. In a bowl, add cream cheese, half of each asiago and parmesan cheese and half of breadcrumbs and whisk till combine.

Mix squash and cheese mixture. Place this mixture in baking dish. Top with remaining cheese and breadcrumbs.

Bake for 15 to 20 minutes or till cheese melt completely.

Serving Suggestions:

Increase the flavor by adding some minced fresh herbs like thyme, rosemary and chives.

Eggplant Lasagna

This amazingly delicious lasagna is suitable for a main meal.

Ingredients:

¼ cup of olive oil
½ cup of onion, chopped
3 cloves of garlic, minced
1 medium eggplant, peeled and cubed
9 lasagna noodles, cooked
1 package of mozzarella cheese, divided
1 (26-ounce) jar of spaghetti sauce
¼ cup of Parmesan cheese

Directions:

Preheat oven to 350 degrees F. Grease a baking dish with cooking spray. In a skillet, heat oil on medium heat.

Add onion, garlic and eggplant. Cook, stirring often for about 15 minutes or till eggplant becomes tender. Keep aside.

Place 3 noodles in prepared baking dish. Place eggplant slices over noodles. Sprinkle mozzarella cheese. Spread spaghetti sauce over cheese. Repeat the layers.

Top with Parmesan and then bake for 40 to 45 minutes.

Serving Suggestions:

Enjoy more by drizzling with some balsamic syrup over lasagna before serving.

Candied Sweet Potato Casserole

This delicious and simple dish will force your family members to clean their plates at dinning table.

Ingredients:

2 pounds of sweet potatoes
2 tablespoons of milk
¼ cup of butter, softened
1 egg
½ cup of granulated sugar
½ teaspoon of vanilla extract
A pinch of salt
½ cup of cornflakes, crushed
½ table spoon of butter, melted
½ tablespoon of brown sugar
2 tablespoons of pecans, chopped
½ cup of miniature marshmallows

Directions:

Preheat oven to 400 degrees F.

Bake sweet potatoes for 1 hour. Keep aside to cool for 20 minutes. Peel and mash them.

Reduce the temperature of oven to 350 degrees F.

Grease a baking dish with cooking spray. Add mashed potatoes, milk, ¼ cup of butter, egg, sugar, vanilla extract and salt in a food processor. Beat on medium speed till smooth. Place potato mixture in baking dish.

In a bowl, mix cornflakes, melted butter, brown sugar and pecans. Place egg mixture over potato mixture in diagonal rows 1 inch apart.

Bake for 30 minutes.

Remove baking dish from oven. Let it stay for 8 minutes. Place the marshmallows in rows between cornflakes mixture.

Bake for 10 minutes more.

Serving suggestions:

Replace granulated sugar with brown sugar if you like less sweetness.

Summer Squash Casserole

Combination of squash, cheese and crackers makes a memorable and zesty main course dish.

Ingredients:

1 ½ tablespoons of butter, divided
2 tablespoons of olive oil
1 cup of onion, chopped
Salt and black pepper, to taste
1 teaspoon of garlic, minced
6 medium zucchini, sliced into thin rounds
6 medium summer squash, sliced into thin rounds
1 teaspoon of fresh thyme leaves, chopped finely
¼ cup of heavy cream
3 large eggs
1 cup of butter crackers, crushed
½ cup of Parmesan cheese, grated

Directions:

Preheat oven to 350 degrees F.

Grease a 9x13-inch casserole dish with ½ tablespoon of butter. In a pan, add oil and remaining butter and heat on medium-high heat.

Add onion, salt and pepper. Sauté for 5 minutes or till onion become tender. Add garlic and sauté for 30 seconds. Now, add zucchini and squash.

Cook, stirring often for about 20 minutes or till vegetables become tender. Stir in thyme leaves. Remove from stove.

With a spoon, place vegetables in casserole dish. Reserve the liquid. In a bowl, add cream, eggs and reserved liquid. Beat well.

Pour the cream mixture over vegetables evenly. Bake for 30 minutes.

Remove casserole dish from oven. Top the casserole with crackers and cheese.

Bake again for 10 to 15 minutes or till it becomes golden brown.

Serving Suggestions:

Enjoy your casserole with cheesy garlic bread.

Layered Cheesy Vegetable Casserole

This tasty and rich cheesy vegetable casserole is irresistible even for non-vegetarians.

Ingredients:

1 tablespoon of canola oil
1 large onion, chopped, finely
1 large green bell pepper, seeded and cubed into 1-inch pieces
½ cup of mushrooms, sliced
1 small eggplant, cubed into 1-inch pieces
1 large tomato, chopped
½ teaspoon of thyme
Salt and black pepper, to taste
1 cup of packed herb seasoned stuffing mix
2 cups of Swiss cheese, shredded and divided

Directions:

Preheat oven to 350 degrees F.

Grease a casserole dish with cooking spray. In a skillet, heat oil on medium heat. Add onion and sauté for 3 minutes. Add bell pepper, mushrooms and eggplant. Cook, stirring continuously for about 3 minutes.

Stir in tomato, thyme, salt and pepper. Spread stuffing mix in prepared casserole dish evenly.

Place half of vegetable mixture. Sprinkle half of cheese. Place a second layer of vegetable mixture over the cheese. Cover and bake for 30 minutes.

After that, remove from oven, top with remaining cheese. Bake for 10 minutes further or till cheese melts.

Serving Suggestions:

For a crispy touch you can sprinkle breadcrumbs just before baking.

Cheesy Potato & Zucchini Casserole

Cheese and potato....surely it will b a favorite dish of kids.

Ingredients:

6 tablespoons of mozzarella cheese, grated
1 ½ tablespoon of fresh cream
½ teaspoon of dried oregano
Salt and black pepper, to taste
2 large potatoes, boiled, peeled and sliced thickly
1 small zucchini, sliced thinly
1 large tomato, sliced thinly

Directions:

Preheat oven to 400 degrees F. Grease a casserole dish with cooking spray.

In a bowl, add cheese, cream, oregano, salt and pepper and mix well. Divide the cheese mixture in three portions.

Place the sliced potatoes in casserole dish evenly. Spread the first portion of cheese mixture on potatoes. Place the sliced zucchini over the potato layer.

Spread the second portion of cheese mixture over zucchini. Place the sliced tomatoes on zucchini layer.

Spread the remaining cheese mixture on top.

Bake for 20 minutes or till cheese melts and it becomes light brown.

Serving Suggestion:

Serve this tasty cheesy casserole with tomato ketchup.

Pasta & White Bean Casserole

A simple do-ahead dish is perfect for potlucks.

Ingredients:

1 cup of orzo pasta
2 tablespoons of extra-virgin olive oil
½ medium red onion, chopped
3 cloves of garlic, minced
1 cup of mushrooms, sliced
1 green bell pepper, sliced
2 cups of spinach, torn
1 (15-ounce) can of cannelloni beans, rinsed and drained
¾ cup of Parmesan cheese, grated and divided
Fresh herbs (basil, parsley and cilantro), chopped for topping

Directions:

Preheat oven to 375 degrees F. Grease a casserole dish with cooking spray.

Add water and salt in a pot and bring to a boil. Add pasta and boil, lessening the time 2 to 3 minutes.

In a skillet, heat oil on medium heat. Sauté onion for 3 to 4 minutes or till it becomes tender. Add garlic and sauté for 30 seconds. Add mushrooms and bell pepper. Cook, stirring often for about 3 minutes. Add spinach and cook till spinach wilts. Reduce heat to low.

Stir in beans, pasta and half of cheese and mix well.

Place pasta mixture in casserole dish evenly.

Sprinkle the remaining cheese on top. Bake for 15 minutes.

While serving, garnish pasta casserole with chopped herbs.

Serving Suggestions:

Tastes best if served with crunchy fresh salad.

Spinach & Rice Casserole

This is absolutely a scrumptious meal.

Ingredients:

2 tablespoons of olive oil, divided
1 large onion, chopped finely
4 cloves of garlic, minced
1 ½ pounds of fresh spinach, chopped
Salt, to taste
2 cups of rice, cooked and fluffed with fork
Black pepper, to taste
¼ teaspoon of cayenne pepper
¼ teaspoon of nutmeg powder
1 teaspoon of yellow mustard
1 cup of milk
2 eggs, beaten
1 cup of cheddar cheese, grated
Paprika, to taste

Directions:

Preheat oven to 350 degrees F. Grease a baking dish with 1 tablespoon of oil.

In a large skillet, heat 1 tablespoon of oil on medium heat. Sauté onion for 5 to 6 minutes till it becomes tender.

Add garlic and sauté for 30 seconds. Add spinach and salt. Cook, stirring for about 5 minutes.

Stir in rice, black pepper, cayenne, nutmeg and mustard. In a small bowl, add milk and eggs and beat well.

Stir in egg mixture and cheese in rice mixture. Place rice mixture in prepared baking dish evenly.

Sprinkle paprika on top. Bake for 35 to 40 minutes or till it become brown on top.

Serving Suggestions:

For a more refreshing flavor you can add some freshly grated lemon zest just before serving.

Black Bean Casserole

This recipe is easy to prepare and tastes excellent.

Ingredients:

1 tablespoon of olive oil
1 cup of onion, chopped
1 pound of canned black beans, rinsed and drained
1 (16-ounce) can of whole kernel corn, drained
4 ½ ounces of yellow cornmeal
1(4-ounce) can of green chilies, drained
1 (16-ounce) can of stewed tomatoes
1 ¼ cups of skimmed milk
2 teaspoons of chili powder
¼ cup of cheddar cheese, shredded

Directions:

Preheat oven to 350 degrees F. Lightly, Grease a baking dish with cooking spray.

In a large bowl, add all ingredients except cheese. Mix properly.

Place bean mixture in prepared baking dish. Spread cheese on top. Bake for 45 minutes.

Serving Suggestions:

Serve this casserole along with fresh chopped scallions, tomatoes and shredded lettuce.

Basil Tomato & Zucchini Casserole

A simple and tasty dish that highlights the flavors of fresh vegetables.

Ingredients:

1 tablespoon of fresh basil, chopped plus extra for topping
1 ½ tablespoons of lemon juice
½ cup of olive oil plus 2 tablespoons
1 ½ pounds of tomatoes, cut into ¼-inch rounds
1 pound of zucchini, cut into ¼-inch rounds
1 cup of onion, chopped
4 cloves of garlic, minced
1 cup of breadcrumbs
Salt and black pepper, to taste

Directions:

Preheat oven to 400 degrees F. Grease a casserole dish.

In a large bowl, add 1 tablespoon of basil, lemon juice, ½ cup of olive oil and ½ teaspoon of salt. Mix all ingredients.

Add tomatoes and zucchini in the same bowl. Marinate for 20 to 30 minutes. Grill the vegetables on preheated grill for 2 minutes per side.

In a pan, heat 2 tablespoons of olive oil on medium heat. Sauté onion and garlic till tender. Remove from heat. Stir in breadcrumbs.

In casserole dish, place the first layer of zucchini. Place a layer of tomatoes on zucchini. Spread onion mixture on vegetables. Sprinkle the salt and pepper. Repeat the layers.

Cover and bake for 15 minutes.

Uncover and bake again for 15 to 20 minutes or till top becomes brown. Top with chopped basil and serve.

Serving Suggestions:

For a much better taste, try garlic olive oil instead of simple olive oil.

Spinach, Potato & Mushrooms Casserole

This dish is a simple layered combination of vegetables and cheese.

Ingredients:

3 pounds of baking potatoes, cut into 1-inch slices
6 tablespoons of olive oil, divided
1 ½ teaspoons of salt, divided
¾ teaspoon of black pepper, divided
4 cloves of garlic, minced
1 medium onion, chopped finely
½ pound of white mushrooms, sliced
1 ½ pound of spinach, stemmed and torn
1 ½ cups of ricotta cheese
½ pound of Gruyere cheese, grated

Directions:

Preheat oven to 400 degrees F. Grease a baking dish.

Add potato, 4 tablespoons of oil, 1 teaspoon of salt, ½ teaspoon of black pepper and garlic. Toss well to coat.

Place potato slices in prepared baking dish. Cover with foil paper. Bake for 30 minutes. Uncover and let them cool.

Meanwhile, in a pan, heat remaining oil on medium heat. Sauté onion till it becomes tender. Add mushrooms and cook for about 5 minutes. Add spinach. Cover and cook till spinach become wilted. Uncover and cook till all liquid is absorbed. Stir in ricotta cheese.

Grease a casserole dish. Divide potatoes and ricotta cheese in 3 portions. Place first layer of potato in casserole dish. Place half of mushrooms mixture on potatoes. Sprinkle first portion of cheese. Repeat the layers.

Top with remaining potatoes and cheese. Bake for 25 minutes.

Serving Suggestions

Give a crispy top to your dish by using crushed cornflakes while baking.

Eggplant, Lentil & Cheese Casserole

Give a little bit different but tasty touch to your lentils in this casserole.

Ingredients:

14 ounces of eggplant, sliced thinly in rounds
Salt and black pepper, to taste
3 tablespoons of vegetable oil
1 red onion, chopped finely
1 clove of garlic, chopped finely
1 red pepper, chopped finely
¼ cup of tomato puree
1 cinnamon stick
1 (14-ounce) can of chopped tomatoes, drained
½ cup of red lentils, cooked (according to package directions)
2 tablespoons of fresh parsley, chopped
½ cup of Greek-style yogurt
2/3 cup of ricotta cheese
1 pinch of nutmeg powder
½ cup of Parmesan cheese, grated

Directions:

Preheat oven to 350 degrees F. Grease a casserole dish.

In a bowl, toss eggplant, salt and pepper. In a pan, heat oil on medium heat. Cook eggplant slices for 2 to 3 minutes per side. Place eggplant slices on a paper towel to drain.

In the same pan, add onion, garlic and red pepper. Cook for 2 to 3 minutes. Pour tomato puree and cook, stirring for 4 to 5 minutes. Add cinnamon stick and tomatoes. Reduce heat to medium-low. Simmer for 4 to 5 minutes. Add lentil and eggplant and simmer for 2 to 3 minutes.

Pour the mixture in prepared casserole dish. Spread chopped parsley on mixture.

In a bowl, mix yogurt, ricotta cheese, nutmeg, salt and black pepper.

Pour yogurt mixture on vegetable mixture. Top with parmesan. Bake for 25 to 30 minutes.

Serving Suggestions:

Serve it with brown rice.

Wild Rice Casserole

It is an impressive and easy side dish to be prepared at the sudden arrival of guests....

Ingredients

3 tablespoons of unsalted butter
8 ounces of white mushrooms, sliced
2 tablespoons of green pepper, minced
4 tablespoon of onion, chopped finely
1 cup of heavy cream
1 can of condensed cream of mushroom soup
¼ teaspoon of dried tarragon
¼ teaspoon of dried basil
1/2 teaspoon of curry powder
Salt and black pepper, to taste
1 cup of wild rice, cooked (according to package directions)

Directions:

Preheat oven to 350 degrees F. Grease a casserole dish.

In a pan, melt butter on medium heat. Add mushrooms, green pepper and onion. Cook for 8 to 10 minutes or till mushrooms become soft.

Add cream, soup, spices and rice. Stir till well mixed.

Place the rice mixture in casserole dish. Bake for 40 to 50 minutes.

Serving Suggestions:

Serve this dish with slivered almonds.

Baked Candied Yam & Apple Casserole

This excellent recipe really tastes like a perfect dessert.

Ingredients:

1 cup of sugar
2 tablespoons pf cornstarch
2 tablespoons of butter
2 cups of orange juice, warm
2 teaspoons of lemon juice
3 large apples, peeled, cored and sliced
4 large yams, boiled, peeled and sliced

Directions:

Preheat oven to 325 degrees F. Grease a casserole dish with butter.

In a bowl, add sugar, cornstarch, butter, orange juice and lemon juice. Mix well.

Place apples and yams in prepared casserole dish. Spread butter sauce on apples and yams.

Cover and bake for 1½ hours.

Serving Suggestions:

Top this sweet casserole with creamy toasted marshmallows.

Vegetarian Mexican Casserole

Great main dish for vegetarian menu…..

Ingredients:

For sauce:

1 can of vegetable broth
1 (16-ounce) can of sour cream
1 medium onion, chopped finely
2 tablespoons of all-purpose flour

For casserole:

3 large onions, diced
2 cans of chilies, diced
2 cups of olives, chopped
12 corn tortillas, divided
3 cups of cheddar cheese, grated and divided

Directions:

Preheat oven to 350 degrees F. Grease a casserole dish with cooking spray.

In a food processor, add all sauce ingredients. Blend till smooth. Keep aside.

In a large bowl, mix onion, chilies and olives. Place half of tortillas in casserole dish.

Place vegetable mixture on tortillas. Spread half of the sauce on vegetables. Sprinkle half of cheese. Again spread remaining tortillas and then remaining sauce. Sprinkle remaining cheese all over the top.

Bake for 30 to 40 minutes.

Serving suggestions:

This casserole really goes well with a bowl of hot Taco soup.

Tortellini Zucchini Casserole

Tortellini and vegetables come together to make a very yummy dinner.

Ingredients:

2 medium zucchini, sliced into ¼-inch thick pieces
1 large onion, sliced thinly
1 large red bell pepper, sliced thinly
1 large green bell pepper, sliced thinly
1 ½ cups of 3 cheese Tortellini, cooked
1 can of tomato bisque
1 can of diced tomatoes
1 (2 ¼-ounce) can of black olives, sliced
1 cup of cheddar cheese, shredded

Directions:

Preheat oven to 350 degrees F. Grease a casserole dish with cooking spray.

In a bowl, mix vegetables.

In second bowl, mix bisque and tomatoes. Place vegetables in casserole dish.

Place tortellini on vegetables. Pour tomato mixture and then sprinkle cheese and olives on top.

Lastly, bake for 45 to 50 minutes.

Serving Suggestions:

It will be great deal if served with salad and garlic bread.

Tater Tot Casserole

This unique and tasty veggie casserole is perfect for family dishes collection.

Ingredients:

2 pounds of tater tots, thawed
1 cup of onion, chopped finely
1 dash of garlic powder
1 (10.5-ounce) can of condensed cream of mushroom soup
1 (16-ounce) can of sour cream
1 cup of butter, softened and divided
½ teaspoon of salt
3 cups of cornflakes
Paprika, to taste
2 tablespoons of Parmesan cheese

Directions:

Preheat oven to 350 degrees F. Grease a casserole dish with cooking spray.

In a large bowl, add tater tots, onion, garlic powder, soup, sour cream, ½ cup of softened butter and salt.

Mix well till combined. In another bowl, mix cornflakes and remaining butter.

In casserole dish, place tater tots mixture. Spread cornflakes mixture on tater tot mixture.

Sprinkle paprika and cheese on top. Bake for 45 to 50 minutes or till it become brown.

Serving Suggestions:

You can add canned and drained greens beans and corn for a richer flavor.

Mexicaly's Corn And Red Bean Casserole

It's A+ delicious dish for everyone. This mixture is sweet and spicy meal to warm the belly during winter cold nights.

Ingredients:

1 tablespoon olive oil
1 medium red onion, minced
2 garlic cloves, minced
1 tbsp. celery stick, minced
½ cup brown sugar
1 teaspoon chili powder
1 teaspoon dried Jalapeno peppers, chopped
1 cup diced fresh red tomatoes
1 cup red kidney beans, drained and rinsed
1 cup corn kernels
1 cup potatoes, cubed
1 red bell pepper, cubed 1"
1 green bell pepper, cubed 1"
1 cup vegetable stock
1 cup soy milk
4 cups of vegetable broth stock
a dash of salt and pepper
½ cup of Parmesan cheese, sliced thinly

Directions:

Heat the oil in a sauté pan over medium heat. Put onions, celery and garlic cook until translucent.

Mix in all the tomatoes, peppers, sugar, herbs and spices. Cook for an additional minute and then transfer to a casserole.

Add all the remaining ingredients and stir to combine- beans, broth, milk, corn and potatoes.

Cook on low heat at 45 minutes or on high for 30 minutes.

Serving suggestions:

Serve in small ramekins with preferred dips such as cheddar cheese, sour cream and sourdough bread.

Vegetarians' White Beans And Spinach With Silk Tofu

This dish for lunch and dinner is rich in protein and nutrients everybody will ask for more servings.

Ingredients:

2 tbsp. corn oil
2 large red onions, chopped
5 cloves garlic, crushed
2 tbsp. celery stick, chopped
1 red bell pepper, cubed 1"
1/2 tsp. fresh dill
¼ tsp. basil, dried
2 cups white beans, boiled and drained
2 cups spinach, washed if needed
2 cups diced tomatoes with juice
5 cups vegetable stock
a dash of salt and pepper
a dash of nutmeg
3 freshly shaved Parmesan, for garnishing

Directions:

Heat the oil in a large heavy frying pan; add the onions, celery, garlic, bell peppers and cook until soft and translucent. Mix all the other ingredients. Sauté' and simmer for 5 minutes.

Spray the casserole with non-stick spray or brush with cooking oil. Place the entire simmered dish into the slow cooker.

Cook for 30 minutes on high heat and 45 minutes on low heat.

Serving suggestion:

Serve in ramekins topped with Parmesan shavings and a dash of nutmeg, salt and pepper. You may serve this delicious hot dish with sourdough bread or steamed rice.

Rainbow Veggie Dish

A colorful and aromatic hot dish best served with your fave bread or pasta everyone will have a warm dinner.

Ingredients:

3 tbps. sesame oil
1 large red onion, minced
2 cloves garlic, crushed
1 tbsp. celery stick, minced
1 red bell pepper, cubed 1"
1 yellow bell pepper, cubed 1"
1 green bell pepper, cubed 1"
1 teaspoon ginger, julienned
1 cinnamon stick
1/4 teaspoon vanilla powder
1/2 teaspoon red cayenne pepper powder
2 large potatoes, diced
1 cup sweet potatoes, peeled and diced
2 large carrots, peeled and dice
1 cup sugar baby pumpkin, peeled, seeded, and dice
6 cups vegetable broth
1/2 cup California raisins
1 cup baby spinach leaves, blanched
1 tablespoon apple cider vinegar
1 tbsp lime juice
1 tbsp. Kosher salt
a dash of salt and pepper

a dash of nutmeg

Directions:

Heat the oil in a casserole over high heat and add the onions until soft and translucent.

Add the garlic, bell pepper, ginger, cinnamon, a pinch of salt and pepper, and all other herbs and spices.

Sauté all the ingredients until soft and fragrant for about 5 minutes.

Add all the root vegetables and broth, simmer it for 10 minutes. Cook until soft for additional 30 minutes.

After it's cooked, add the baby spinach and raisins, season with salt and pepper gently stir.

Serving suggestion:

Serve in soup bowl with small ramekins, with cheese bread, pasta noodles or steamed Quinoa.

Cabbage, Lentil & Potato Casserole

This is a nutritious vegetable dish with aromatic flavor and taste. Easy to cook and ready to eat in minutes

Ingredients

2 tbsp. corn oil
1 tbsp. olive oil
2 garlic cloves, minced
1 red onion, chopped
1 celery stalk, minced
1 yellow bell peppers, seeded, cut into 1" cubes
1 large potato, cubed
1 medium carrot, sliced
1 cup garbanzos, boiled and rinsed
1 cup dried brown lentils,
1 cup cabbage leaves cut in 2"
2 pcs fried tofu, cut into big squares
5 cups vegetable broth
3 tbsp soy sauce
2 tbsp white/red wine
¼ tsp dried thyme
¼ tsp dried dill
¼ tsp dried cayenne powder
¼ tsp dried basil
3 chives, chopped
2 tbsp soy or almond flour, for thickening
salt and pepper to taste

Directions:

Heat the oil in a large casserole over high heat. Add onion, celery, carrot, garlic. Cover and simmer until softened, about 5 minutes, stirring occasionally.

Add all the vegetables, lentils, potatoes, broth, clear sauce, herbs, spices and all other ingredients (except the cabbage leaves). Stir to combine. Cover and cook on high heat for 15 minutes.

Place the cabbage leaves in boiling water and cook until tender. Drain well and stir into stew. Season it with Tabasco sauce, salt and pepper to taste.

Serving suggestion:

Serve in a soup bowl with steamed Couscous, rice or wheat bread.

Hot And Sweet Potatoes With Fried Tofu Squares

Sweet and spicy hot dish everyone will love and get for more servings.

Ingredients:

1/4 cup corn oil
2 cloves garlic, chopped
1 Jalapeño chilis, seeded and minced
1 red onion, chopped
1 tsp ginger, grated
2 large potatoes, cut into 1 inch cubes
1 cup sweet yellow potatoes, cut into 1 inch cubes
2 Tofu squares, cut into 2" and deep-fried
6 cups broth

Herbs and spices:

1/2 Tbsp ground red chili pepper
1/2 Tsp ground cumin
1 Tbsp garam masala
1 Tbsp Kosher salt
1 Tbsp whole peppercorns

Toppings: (add at the last part of cooking)

2 Tbsp Couscous
2 Tbsp almond flour

½ cup peanuts, chopped

Directions:

Sauté all the ingredients all together, except the toppings, herbs and spices. Mix once. Simmer for 5 minutes.

Place in casserole dish.

Add in the almond flour, herbs and spices. Mix and stir once again. Simmer and cover for 15 minutes. Cook at 300 degrees for 20 minutes.

Serving suggestion:

Serve topped with cooked couscous and chopped peanuts. Serve with your fresh vegetable salad or pita bread.

"Tres" (3) Mushroom Casserole

This dish calls for three kinds of mushrooms. But the cook may choose other variety of mushrooms to enjoy this delicious recipe.

Ingredients:

½ cup extra virgin olive oil
3 cloves garlic, minced
1 cup diced red onions
1 Jalapeño pepper, seeded and chopped
1 red bell pepper, seeded and cubed
1 yellow bell pepper, seeded and cubed
1 cup sliced baby Portobello mushrooms
1 cup sliced button mushrooms
1 cup sliced Oyster mushrooms
1 cup corn kernels, drained
½ cup cooked red beans, drained
½ cup green olives
½ cup green capers
1 tsp Kosher salt (or sea salt)
½ tsp ground black pepper
½ tsp paprika
2 tsp chili powder
5 pcs small fresh basil leaves
½ cup grated mozzarella cheese
½ cup chopped walnuts

Directions:

Sauté in a casserole the onions, garlic, jalapeño and bell pepper with olive oil until soft.

Add in the mushrooms, corn kernels and red beans. Cover and boil for 5 minutes.

Stir in the remaining ingredients except walnuts. Cover and on low heat for 5 minutes

Serving suggestion:

Transfer to serving dish and topped it with ground walnuts and basil leaves. Serve it with fried or steamed tofu.

Stuffed Bell Peppers With Soy Sauce

This new recipe is easily prepared and even kids can concoct with fun.

Ingredients:

4 large red bell peppers, seeded and cored
4 large green bell peppers, seeded and cored
4 large yellow bell peppers, seeded and cored

Stuffing:

2 cups garbanzos, cooked and mashed
2 eggs, boiled, shelled and crumbled
1 cup crumbled silken tofu
1 cup grated Mozzarella cheese
¼ cup Quinoa, steamed
1 large white onions, minced
½ teaspoon dried thyme
½ teaspoon salt and freshly ground pepper
a pinch of garlic salt for every bell pepper
½ cup olive oil (for drizzling)

Sauce:

1 cup soy sauce
1 tbsp cornstarch
2 tbsp cold water

Toppings:

a pinch of nutmeg for every bell pepper
a pinch of cinnamon powder for every bell pepper
a pinch of roasted sesame seeds for every bell pepper

Directions:

Remove the core and seeds of the bell peppers. Slice a thin layer from the base of each bell pepper so they stand flat on platters. Slice off tops just below stem and discard stems. Wash with cold water. Drain and remove excess water. Cover. Set aside.

Mix all the stuffing ingredients-eggs, beans, garbanzos, cheese, Quinoa, herbs and flavoring in a bowl. Season with salt and pepper and mix well. Set aside and cover.

Mix and whisk the soy sauce, cold water and cornstarch. Simmer for 2 minutes.

Fill the cored peppers with prepared mixture. Place upright the bell peppers in the casserole and drizzle with olive oil. Bake in low heat for 20 minutes.

Pour the soy sauce before serving.

Serving suggestion:

Sprinkle stuffed peppers with a pinch of toppings and serve with lemon wedges. Serve with deep fried or steamed salmon or tofu.

Mediterranean Casserole

A bunch of potatoes and pumpkin with herbs and spices will warm anyone's cold belly.

Ingredients:

2 tbsp olive oil
3 cloves garlic, chopped
1 cup chopped onion
1 cup sweet potatoes, peeled and cubed 1"
1 cup pumpkin - peeled, seeded and cubed 1"
1 cup cubed eggplant
1 cup pears, peeled and cubed 1"
1 carrot, cut into chunks
2 ripe beefsteak tomatoes, cubed 1"
3 cups vegetable broth
½ cup raisins, finely chopped
2 tsp. Kosher salt
¼ teaspoon ground cayenne
¼ teaspoon ground nutmeg
¼ teaspoon paprika
5 pcs fresh basil leaves

Add on the last part of cooking:

½ cup silken tofu, crumbled
½ cup walnuts, shelled
½ cup chopped pecans

Directions:

Sauté the onions and garlic in olive oil until soft. Add in all the main ingredients. Simmer for 15 minutes or until potatoes and pumpkins are soft.

Add a cup or more of broth if the dish gets dried.

Mix the silken tofu. Simmer for a minute. Then transfer into a serving dish.

Serving suggestion:

Drizzle with chopped nuts. Serve hot with Quinoa or rye bread.

Spicy-Sweet Pumpkin And Eggplant Lasagne

Try this new lasagna recipe with the sweet and zesty taste of pears and apples.

Ingredients:

2 tbsp corn oil
2 red onions, chopped
4 garlic cloves, chopped
3 cups diced red tomatoes
2 cups tomato sauce
5 cups pumpkin, pureed
5 cups eggplants, cut in 3" and fried
1 cup red apples, cubed
1 cup pears, cubed
1 cup broth
3 tbsp brown sugar
¼ tsp dried rosemary
¼ tsp oregano powder
5 leaves of basil, chopped
2 branches of dill, chopped leaves
1 tsp red hot chili pepper, chopped
1 tsp paprika
¼ teaspoon ground nutmeg
1 cup Mozzarella cheese
½ tsp Kosher salt

Pasta ingredients: (Boil together)

12 pcs Lasagna noodles, boiled and drained
6 cups water
a pinch of salt
2 tbsp cooking oil

Directions:

Heat the corn oil and add the onions and garlic until soft. Add the tomatoes and simmer for 5 minutes.

Add and simmer all the ingredients for 5 minutes. Set aside

Boil and cook the lasagna ingredients for 5 minutes.

Brush the bottom part of the casserole with cooking oil or cooking spray.

Place the lasagna on the casserole and spread ½ cup of the mixture. Layer the lasagna with half cheese mixture. Repeat the layering according to your preference.

Sprinkle with the mozzarella. Bake on low heat for 30 minutes.

Serving suggestion

Serve hot with French bread and clear onion soup.

Bread And Chickpeas Curry Casserole

This is the practical way to have a delicious dish with day old bread and leftovers. Spice it up with this new yummy recipe.

Ingredients:

3 tablespoons corn oil
2 tablespoons annato oil
¼ cup celery stick, chopped
1 chopped white onions, medium
5 garlic cloves, crushed
1 small yellow bell pepper, cubed
1 cups carrot, cubed
1 cup cooked chickpeas (garbanzo beans)
1 cup bread, cubed (day old or leftover)
1 cup leftover food, cubed
1 tablespoon curry powder
¼ tsp turmeric powder
1 teaspoon grated peeled fresh ginger
½ tablespoon paprika
2 Serrano chilli, seeded and minced
3 teaspoons brown sugar
3 teaspoons honey
1 teaspoon salt
3 cups vegetable broth
2 cups fresh baby spinach leaves
1 cup coconut milk

Directions:

Heat the oil with onion, garlic and celery until soft. Add all the ingredients (except spinach and coconut milk) and simmer for 5 minutes.

Add the spinach and coconut milk. Cover and cook on high for 20 minutes until vegetables are tender and sauce thickens.

Serving suggestion:

Drizzle with honey and Tabasco sauce. Serve hot with steamed Japanese rice or pita bread.

Tofu Squares And Mushrooms With Angel's Pasta

The pasta sauce base is great as rice toppings aside from pasta noodles. This tasty dish can be enjoyed by your lunch or dinner guests.

Ingredients:

Veggie Ingredients:

5 pcs tofu squares, quartered and deep fried
1 chopped onion
1 tbsp cooking oil
1 cup of cubed button mushrooms
1 cup of cubed Portobello mushrooms
1 cup cubed carrots
5 chopped French green beans
2 cups torn baby spinach leaves
3 pcs. fresh basil leaves, finely chopped
1 tsp ground white pepper
2 cups red fresh tomatoes, cubed
5 sun-dried tomatoes, finely chopped
1 cup tomato sauce
1 tsp Kosher salt

Veggie-cheese mixture:

½ cup shredded mozzarella cheese
¼ cup shredded cheddar cheese
¼ cup silken tofu, crumbled
1 large egg, lightly beaten
½ cup shaved fresh Parmesan cheese (for garnishing)
Cooking spray or 1 tbsp cooking oil
1 Package of Angelhair Pasta

Directions:

Deep fry the tofu squares. Drain and set aside.

Sauté the onions with cooking oil until translucent. Add all the veggie ingredients and simmer for 10 minutes. Set aside once cooked.

In a separate bowl, combine and whisk all the cheese and beaten eggs. Stir in the silken tofu, and set aside.

Spread 1 cup pasta sauce veggie mixture in the bottom of a casserole coated with cooking spray or brush with cooking oil. Pour half of the angel's pasta noodles over sauce mixture.

Layer a cup of cheese mixture and a cup veggie mixture over the noodles. Repeat the layers, ending with cheese mixture. Sprinkle with the shaved Parmesan. Cover with lid and bake for 30 minutes or until the cheese melted.

Serving suggestion:

Transfer on a pasta platter and put the fried tofu while hot. Serve immediately.

Stuffed Lettuce Rolls With Nuts And Berries

A yummy easy recipe packed with freshness and vitamins.

Ingredients:

5-6 pcs fresh lettuce leaves, washed and drained
2 tablespoon corn oil
½ cup finely chopped onion
¼ cup finely chopped garlic
1 cup cooked Couscous
2 cups crumbled feta cheese
1 cup crumbled silk tofu
3 tablespoons pine nuts, toasted
2 tablespoons walnuts, toasted and chopped
2 tablespoons pecans, toasted and chopped
1 tablespoons peanuts, toasted and chopped
¼ cup fresh raspberries
¼ cup sultana raisins
1 tsp cinnamon powder
½ teaspoon salt
¼ teaspoon freshly ground black pepper
2 tbsp white wine

Flavouring:

½ cup fresh orange juice
2 tablespoons brown sugar

Directions:

Cut off hard portion of each lettuce leaf. Wash and drain. Set leaves aside.

Heat the casserole with corn oil and sauté onions and garlic until soft. Add all the ingredients, nuts, berries, herbs and spices. Simmer for 5 minutes. Set aside to cool.

Mix the flavoring ingredients- orange juice and sugar in a saucepan. Cover and simmer for 5 minutes until it thickens.

Place lettuce leaves on a flat surface and fill with a tablespoon of nuts and berries mixture into the center. Fold in edges of leaves over mixture. Roll up.

Arrange the rolls on a platter and pour the flavoring sauce.

Serving suggestion:

Serve with your favorite pasta, stew or clear soup.

Breadfruit And White Beans Casserole

A savoury dish recipe that tastes like baked bread packed with nutrients and vitamins. Serve anytime of the day for a filling meal.

Ingredients:

2 tablespoons corn oil
½ cup chopped onions
½ cup chopped celery stick
2 garlic cloves, minced
½ cups carrot, cubed 1"
1 cup breadfruit, blanched and cubed 1"
1 cup cooked white beans, drained
3 cups broth
1 teaspoon fresh dill leaves, shredded
2 leaves fresh basil leaves, chopped
¼ tsp nutmeg
¼ tsp paprika
¼ teaspoon garlic salt
¼ teaspoon freshly ground black pepper
½ cup dry breadcrumbs
¼ cup grated fresh Parmesan cheese
2 tablespoons vegan butter
2 links meatless Italian sausage, chopped
a dash of salt and pepper to taste

Directions:

Heat corn oil in a casserole over high heat. Add and sauté onions, carrots, celery and garlic for 3 minutes or until translucent.

Add in all the ingredients, mix and simmer for 10-15 minutes covered with a lid. Cook until sauce thickens.

Transfer the cooked dish into serving bowl.

Serving suggestion:

Sprinkle with chopped parsley, roasted sesame seeds and a dash of nutmeg. Can be eaten with your favorite sourdough bread or steamed pandan rice.

Pumpkin-Parsnip With Apples Casserole

You'll love this recipe with the zesty taste of apples and lemons added. Everybody will ask for take-home treat!

Ingredients:

2 cups pumpkin, peeled and cubed
2 cups chopped parsnip, cubed
1 cup sweet potato, cubed
1 pc chopped peeled Granny Smith apple
1 pc cubed pears
¼ cup lemon juice
1/2 cup chopped sweet white onions
1 stalk celery, minced
2 cups soy milk
2 cups vegan broth
1 cup coconut milk
1 teaspoon cracked black pepper
1/4 teaspoon salt
2 tablespoons vegan whipping cream
1/8 teaspoon paprika
1/8 teaspoon cumin
1 tbsp of chopped leeks

Directions:

Prepare and clean all the vegetables. Cut accordingly. Prepare all the other ingredients.

Combine all the ingredients and mix in a clean bowl. Transfer into the casserole. Cover, stir occasionally and simmer for 35-40 minutes.

Transfer the cooked mixture into the serving bowl.

Serving suggestion:

Sprinkle with a dash of salt and pepper. Can be eaten with your favorite salad, steamed rice or pasta.

Lentil-Tomato Curry

This new recipe is appetizing and easy to cook. You may add your last night's leftover food and it will be more flavourful with some pungent spices available in your pantry.

Ingredients:

1 tbsp sesame oil
1 tbsp annatto oil
1 pc chopped red onion
3 garlic cloves, finely chopped
5 cups vegetable broth
1 cup dried lentils
½ cup garbanzos
½ cup chopped carrot
1 tbsp chopped celery stick
1 pc medium red bell pepper, cubed 1"
½ tsp cayenne powder
1 teaspoon curry powder
1 teaspoon turmeric powder
½ teaspoon ground ginger root
2 cups red tomatoes, cubed
5 pcs. vegan Italian sausages, sliced thinly
a dash of salt and pepper
a dash of roasted sesame seeds

Directions:

Heat canola and annatto oil directly in the casserole and sauté onions, celery and garlic until soft. Add the sausages and sauté for 5 minutes.

Add all the ingredients and simmer for 25-30 minutes until beans are soft and sauce thickens.

Ladle the curry on small ramekin bowls.

Serving suggestion:

Sprinkle with a dash of paprika and Tabasco sauce. Can be eaten with your favorite newly baked croissant or pasta.

Brown Rice With Veggie Casserole

This is a nutritious complete meal with rice and viand in one. Easy to cook and filling for the young active kids too.

Ingredients:

1 tbsp corn oil
1 tbsp sesame oil
½ cup chopped onions
1 tbsp celery stick
½ cup minced carrots
½ cup minced raisins
1 tbsp chopped garlic
1 cup brown rice, washed and drained
1 cup green peas, rinsed and drained
3 pcs dried Shiitake mushrooms, sliced thinly
1 package extra-firm tofu, drained and cubed
1/2 cup roasted red bell peppers, cubed 1"
1/2 cup small broccoli florets
1/2 cup cabbage leaves, sliced thinly
1/2 cup shredded chicken fillets, skin removed
3 cups broth

Add at the last part of cooking and just before serving:

1 tsp curry powder
1 tablespoon grated peeled fresh ginger

2 tablespoons brown sugar or molasses
1 teaspoon Kosher salt
¼ tablespoon chopped fresh dill leaves
¼ tablespoon chopped fresh basil leaves

Directions:

Sauté the onions, garlic, carrots and celery with corn and sesame oil. Add all the ingredients and simmer for 20 minutes in a big casserole.

Add in the last ingredients to flavor the dish. Cook further at 5 minutes until brown rice is tender and sticky.

Transfer the rice dish on serving platter. Sprinkle with a dash of salt and pepper.

Serving suggestion:

Serve hot and can be eaten with your favorite hot cocoa or wine and a baked salmon on the side.

Manila Red Beans And Rice Casserole

Rice meals are perfect match for busy moms and working people to fill their day with this easy-to-cook dish.

Ingredients:

2 tablespoons corn oil
1 tsp annatto oil
1 tsp sesame oil
3 cloves garlic, crushed
1/2 cup chopped onion
1 pc small chopped red bell pepper
1 pc small chopped green bell pepper
1 cup dried red beans, washed and drained
1 cup dried red rice, washed and drained
2 cups fresh coconut water
2 cups coconut milk
1 cup vegetable broth
1 teaspoon salt
1 teaspoon chopped ginger root
1 teaspoons fresh basil leaves, chopped
1 pc green chilli, minced
2 tbsp hot pepper sauce
2 tbsp fish sauce
2 tbsp soy sauce

Directions:

Boil the beans for 15-20 minutes. Drain and set aside.

In a casserole sauté the onions, garlic and bell peppers with corn, annatto and sesame oil until soft. Ensure to sauté the condiments with the oil to achieve flavor and aroma. Add the cooked beans, rice and all the other ingredients.

Cook the rice mixture for 20-25 minutes or until soft and slightly sticky.

You may serve the casserole directly on the table or transfer to a serving dish. Sprinkle it with some hot sauce, a dash of salt and cayenne.

Serving suggestion:

Serve hot and can be eaten with your favorite fresh vegetable salad or a baked prawns on the side.

Couscous, Beans And Corn Burritos

Packed with protein and carbohydrates, active parents will surely love this delicious treat.

Filling Ingredients:

1 cup uncooked couscous
½ cup black-eyed peas
1 cup whole corn kernels
2 cups organic vegetable broth or chicken broth
2 pcs chopped white onions
2 garlic clove, minced
1 tbsp fresh lemon juice
1 teaspoon fresh orange juice
½ teaspoon chopped red pepper
½ teaspoon ground black peppercorns
a dash of ground cumin
½ teaspoon chili powder
1 cup diced tomatoes
¼ cup chopped fresh cilantro

Burrito (or Tortilla) ingredients:

5 (8-inch) flour tortillas or burrito wraps
1 cup vegan cheese, grated
3 cups thinly sliced lettuce
1 cup silken tofu, steam and crumbled

Directions:

Place all the filling ingredients (except the couscous) in a casserole .Cover and simmer for 45 minutes or until beans is tender and liquid is absorbed.

Mixed and add ¼ cup cilantro and couscous at the last 2 minutes of cooking.

Heat the tortillas or burrito wraps according to package directions.

Fill each tortilla with ½ cup filling mixture at the center. Sprinkle with 1tablespoon vegan cheese, tofu and lettuce.

Roll up each tortilla.

Serving suggestion:

Serve with salsa and sour cream. Best side dish with avocado, cucumber and tomato salad.

Black Eyed Peas With Mushroom Casserole

This is a yummy concoction that could be stewed by young teens. Moms and Dads will love it too!

Ingredients:

2 cups dried black-eyed peas, rinsed
1 cup button mushrooms, sliced
1 cup Shiitake mushrooms, thinly sliced
½ cup corn kernels
2 tablespoons olive oil
2 tablespoons sesame oil
1 tablespoon vegan butter
2 medium onions, chopped
2 cloves garlic, minced
2 tsp chipotles
½ cup red bell peppers, cubed 1"
1/4 tablespoon chilli powder
1/4 tablespoon paprika
½ teaspoon cumin seeds or ground cumin
½ teaspoon nutmeg
1 cup fresh coconut water
1 cup coconut milk
2 cups broth
1/2 cup grated vegan cheese

Directions:

Boil the beans until cooked and soft. Drain. Set aside

Sauté the onions, garlic and bell peppers until translucent in a casserole. Add the cooked beans and simmer for 5 minutes.

Mix in all the ingredients, except the cheese. Stir once and simmer for 20-25 minutes more.

Transfer the stew on a dish bowl. Top with vegan cheese.

Serving Suggestion:

Garnish with cheese, a dollop of sour cream and a dash of paprika. Serve with fried bananas or sweet potatoes.

5 S-T-A-R Veggie Casserole

This easy to follow recipe has 5 main ingredients that the entire family will love to eat anytime of the day.

Ingredients:

1 cup Kale greens, cut lengthwise thinly
1 cup brussel sprouts, cut in half
½ cup mung beans, washed and drained
2 pcs Shiitake mushrooms, slice thinly
½ cup tofu fillets, slice thinly
1 tablespoon corn oil
1 cup water
½ teaspoon salt and pepper to taste

Directions:

In a small casserole, stir-fry the tofu strips and brussel sprouts in corn oil until tender and brown.

Stir in the mushrooms and water. Let it simmer for 5 minutes. Mix the kale greens and mung beans. Simmer for additional 3 minutes.

Serving suggestion:

Serve in serving plate topped with roasted sesame seeds and maple syrup. Enjoy with your favorite pasta or risotto!

Honey Sweet Potato's Stew

A hearty stew for autumn and winter, you may crave for second servings. Sweet potato is rich and sweet in flavor and available all-year round. Young teens could whip this creamy dish.

Ingredients:

5 cups sweet potatoes, roasted, peeled and cubed 1"
1 cup potatoes, cubed 1"
½ cup carrots, cubed 1"
¼ cup red kidney beans, boiled and drain
½ cup diced fresh ripe beefsteak tomatoes
5 pcs ripe red cherry tomatoes, whole
1 cup vegan meat, ground or finely chopped
2 pcs vegan sausages, slice thinly
1 cup prawns, shelled
2 cups coconut milk
2 cups coconut water
1 tablespoon canola oil
1 teaspoon sesame oil
1 teaspoon chopped garlic
1 teaspoon chopped onions
1 pc medium red bell pepper
1 tablespoon balsamic vinegar
1 tablespoon brown sugar
½ teaspoon paprika
½ teaspoon salt and pepper to taste

Directions:

In a small casserole, saute' the garlic, bell peppers and onions with in canola and sesame oil until soft. Mix in the vegan meat, sausages, sweet potatoes and potatoes stirring for 5 minutes.

Combine in all ingredients- prawns, tomatoes, coconut milk, water, seasonings and herbs. Stir once. Cover and simmer for 20 minutes until soft and sauce thickens.

Serving suggestion:

Put the hot stew in a big bowl and you may drizzle it with some maple syrup. Enjoy with your favorite wheat wraps or tortilla chips.

Sweet Hearty Fruit-Veggie Stew

This 3-step mouth-watering healthy stew recipe will be one of your favorite side dishes, fresh and easy to prepare.

Ingredients:

1 pc medium banana heart, cut into squares 2"
1 pc medium red apple, cube 1"
1 pc medium ripe pears, cube 1"
2 cups baby spinach leaves
2 pcs tofu squares, deep fried
½ cup chopped mixed veggie nuts
½ cup peanut butter
2 tablespoons peanut oil
1 cup coconut water
1 cup coconut milk
2 tablespoons brown sugar
a dash of salt and pepper
1 tsp fresh dill
a pinch of mint powder
a pinch of cayenne

Directions:

In a small casserole, spread the peanut oil evenly. Put the banana heart layered with apples and pears. Simmer with coconut water for 5 minutes.

Mix in all the ingredients (except baby spinach leaves) and stir once. Cover and simmer for 20 minutes. Add the baby spinach leaves and stir.

Serving suggestion:

Transfer to a serving platter and drizzle with Parmesan cheese. Serve immediately. Best serve with your favorite pizza or guacamole salad.

Couscous And Veggie Burger Stew

Who would think that vegetables and grains can be made into yummy burgers? Try this new recipe packed with vitamins and surely mouth-watering.

Ingredients:

1/2 cup Couscous
1/2 cup water (for Couscous mix)
1 teaspoon vegan margarine (for Couscous mix)
1 cup prawns, shelled and finely chopped
1 cup pineapple tidbits, drained and finely chopped
¼ cup chopped carrots
¼ cup chopped celery stick
¼ cup chopped potatoes
¼ cup chopped white
¼ cup chopped red onions
¼ cup chopped pine nuts
¼ cup chopped dried fruits
2 pcs large eggs, beaten
5 tablespoons almond flour
2 tablespoons corn oil, mix with the burger
1 cup corn oil, for frying

Sauce:

1 cup coconut milk

2 tablespoons brown sugar
2 tablespoons corn syrup
1 tablespoon maple syrup
¼ tsp powdered sage
¼ tsp powdered chili
¼ tsp powdered white peppercorns
¼ tsp Kosher salt

Directions:

In a casserole, boil the water. Remove from heat and mix in the couscous with vegan margarine using a fork. Fluff the couscous mix for 2 minutes. Set aside.

Mix all the other ingredients in a separate bowl- prawns, veggies, nuts and fruits(except the sauce mix). Add in the beaten eggs, almond flour and couscous. Mix well.

Form into 10-12 golf-size balls. Heat oil in a pan and fry the mixture. Flatten the balls into burger patties. Fry until cooked on both sides, crispy and brown. Set aside.

In a small saucepan, heat the coconut oil for 3 minutes. Add in and stir constantly the sauce ingredients. Simmer for 2 minutes.

In a casserole, arrange the fried veggie burgers. Pour the sauce mixture and simmer for 3-5 minutes.

Serving suggestion:

Transfer to a platter and serve immediately with a glass of wine, wheat buns or mixed greens.

Baked Potato Pockets With Nutty Pineapple Stew

This potato pockets are packed with nutrients that energize the eaters all day long. You may use leftover tidbits as filling. Make this yummy and mouth-watering recipe on a weekend, and then freeze it to reheat later.

Ingredients:

8 pieces big potatoes, unpeeled and baked
2 tablespoons peanut oil
1 tablespoon corn oil

Season and cover with:

½ teaspoon paprika
¼ teaspoon finely chopped fresh red chillis
2 pcs fresh basil leaves, chopped finely
½ teaspoon chopped fresh dill
a dash of salt and pepper to taste for each potato

Stuffing:

2-3 cups mashed potatoes, from baked potatoes
¼ cup chopped white onions
¼ cup chopped celery sticks
¼ cup chopped pineapple tidbits
¼ cup chopped cashews
¼ cup crumbled tofu
¼ cup button mushrooms chopped finely

¼ cup vegan bacon strips, chopped finely
¼ cup grated Parmesan cheese
¼ cup grated Mozarella cheese
¼ tsp cinnamon powder
2 tbsp. corn oil

Directions:

Prior to cooking clean the unpeeled potatoes in water and salt. Rinse with water twice. Soak in water to remove dirt atleast 1 hour before cooking. Pat it dry.

Pre-heat oven at 350° F. Cut and make a slit along the potatoes horizontally to make pockets. Do not cut through, be cautious not to halve it. Mix and pour the oil, herbs and spices on the potatoes. Drizzle with peanut oil. Add a dash of salt and pepper to taste.

Cover the potatoes individually in aluminum foil. Put in a medium casserole and bake for 25 minutes in high heat.

While baking the potatoes, heat the cooking oil in a separate small casserole. Saute' the onions, mushrooms and vegan bacon until soft. Saute' all the stuffing ingredients for 5 more minutes. Set aside.

Remove the aluminum foil. Cool and core the baked potatoes, leaving a hole as pockets.

Mash the potatoes. Combine with the stuffing mixture.

Stuff the potato pockets with the filling. Sprinkle with a dash of cinnamon or nutmeg.

Serving suggestion:

Transfer on a flat serving platter. Enjoy it as is with your fave hot cocoa drink and soup .

Stuffed Eggplants With Apples Casserole

These stuffed eggplants with apples and nuts are packed with carbohydrates and protein that energize the food gourmets all day long. It's easy to cook and prepare.

Ingredients:

8-10 pieces big and plump purple eggplants, unpeeled, cut lengthwise and baked
3 tablespoons peanut oil
2 tablespoon corn oil

Season and cover with:

¼ teaspoon paprika
2 pcs fresh basil leaves, chopped finely
½ teaspoon curry powder
a dash of salt and pepper to taste for each eggplant

Stuffing:

3-4 cups mashed eggplants, from baked eggplants
2 cups red apples, minced
1 cup water chestnuts, cooked and finely chopped
¼ cup chopped yellow onions
¼ cup chopped yellow bell pepper
2 pcs vegan Italian sausage, finely chopped
¼ cup vegan bacon strips, chopped finely
¼ cup crumbled feta cheese

¼ cup minced Brie cheese
¼ cup grated Mozarella cheese
¼ tsp nutmeg
1 tbsp. annato oil
2 tbsp. sesame oil

Directions:

Pre-heat oven at 350° F. Cut and make a slit along the eggplants horizontally t. Mix and pour the oil, herbs and spices on the eggplants. Drizzle with peanut oil. Add a dash of salt and pepper to taste.

Cover the eggplants individually in aluminum foil. Put in a large casserole and bake for 20 minutes in high heat.

While baking the eggplants, heat the cooking oil in a separate small casserole. Saute' the onions, peppers, vegan bacon and sausages until soft and browned. Add in and saute' all the stuffing ingredients for 5 more minutes. Set aside.

Remove the aluminum foil. Cool and core the baked eggplants, leaving a hole as pockets.

Mash the baked eggplants. Combine with the stuffing mixture.

Stuff the eggplant pockets with the filling. Sprinkle with a dash of nutmeg and your favorite cheese.

Serving suggestion:

Transfer on a flat serving platter. Enjoy it eating with your fave hot ginger tea and macaroni soup .

Stuffed Pumpkin With Chestnuts Casserole

These stuffed eggplants with apples and nuts are packed with carbohydrates and protein that energize the food gourmets all day long. It's easy to cook and prepare.

Ingredients:

8 pieces small plump baby pumpkins, unpeeled and baked
5 tablespoon corn oil

Season and cover with:

¼ teaspoon cumin
¼ teaspoon nutmeg
½ teaspoon curry powder
2 pcs fresh basil leaves, chopped finely
a dash of salt and pepper to taste for each pumpkin

Stuffing:

4 -5 cups mashed pumpkin, from baked pumpkin
1 cup chestnuts, roasted, shelled and finely chopped
¼ cup chopped walnuts
1 cup ripe pears, minced
¼ cup chopped red onions
¼ cup chopped green bell pepper
3 pcs vegan Italian sausage, finely chopped

¼ cup vegan bacon strips, chopped finely
¼ cup minced Brie cheese
¼ cup grated Mozarella cheese
¼ tsp nutmeg
¼ tsp cinnamon powder
1 tbsp. peanut oil
2 tbsp. sesame oil
Sauce: (mix together)
1 cup coconut milk
½ cup brown sugar

Directions:

Pre-heat oven at 350° F. Cut the top of the the pumpkins horizontally . Set that aside as a topper later. Core and remove the seeds.

Mix and pour the oil, herbs and spices on the pumpkins. Drizzle more with corn oil to make it more flavorful with the herbs and spices. The taste will stick to it more. Add a dash of salt and pepper to taste.

Cover the pumpkins individually in aluminum foil. Put in a large casserole and bake for 30 minutes in high heat.

While baking the pumpkins, heat the cooking oil in a separate small casserole. Saute' the onions, nuts, peppers, vegan bacon and sausages until soft and browned. Add in and saute' all the stuffing ingredients for 5 more minutes. Set aside.

Remove the aluminum foil. Cool and core the baked pumpkins , leaving a hole as pockets.

Mash the baked pumpkins. Combine with the stuffing mixture.

Stuff the pumpkins pockets with the filling. Place the pumpkins in a casserole. Pour the mixed coconut milk and sugar. Simmer for 5 minutes or until sauce thickens.

Sprinkle with a dash of nutmeg and your favorite cheese.

Serving suggestion:

Transfer on a flat serving platter. It goes well with your fave hot tea and soup .

Stuffed Beefsteak Tomatoes With Fruit Casserole

These stuffed tomatoes are packed with vitamins and protein that energize the guests all day long. It's easy to cook and mouth-watering!

Ingredients:

5-6 pieces large plump beefsteak tomatoes, unpeeled and baked
5 tablespoon corn oil

Season and cover with:

¼ teaspoon paprika
¼ teaspoon sage
¼ teaspoon turmeric powder
5 pcs fresh basil leaves
a dash of salt and pepper to taste for each

Stuffing:

1-2 cups mashed tomatoes, from baked tomatoes
½ cup red apples, minced
¼ cup chopped pineapple tidbits
¼ cup chopped raisins
¼ cup chopped red maraschino cherries
1 cup chestnuts, roasted, shelled and finely chopped
¼ cup chopped cashew nuts
¼ cup chopped celery

¼ cup chopped green bell pepper
2 pcs vegan Italian sausage, finely chopped
¼ cup vegan ham, chopped finely
¼ cup minced Brie cheese
¼ cup grated Mozarella cheese
¼ tsp cinnamon powder
1 tbsp. peanut oil
2 tbsp. sesame oil
Sauce: (mix and boil together)
1 cup coconut milk
½ cup brown sugar
½ cup maple syrup

Directions:

Pre-heat oven at 350° F. Cut the top of the the tomatoes horizontally . Set that aside as a topper later. Core and remove the seeds.

Mix and pour the oil, herbs and spices on the tomatoes. Drizzle more with corn oil to make it more flavorful with the herbs and spices. The taste will stick to it more. Add a dash of salt and pepper to taste.

Put the tomatoes in a large casserole and bake for 30 minutes in low heat.

While baking the tomatoes, heat the cooking oil in a separate small casserole. Saute' the bell pepper, nuts, fruits, vegan ham and sausages until soft and browned. Add in and saute' all the stuffing ingredients for 5 more minutes. Set aside.

Cool and core the baked tomatoes, leaving a hole for stuffing.

Mash the baked tomatoes. Combine with the stuffing mixture.

Stuff the tomato pockets with the filling. Place the tomatoes in a casserole. Pour the mixed coconut milk, maple syrup and brown sugar. Simmer for 5 minutes or until sauce thickens.

Sprinkle with a dash of cinnamon or vanilla powder and your favorite cheese.

Serving suggestion:

Transfer on a flat serving platter. It goes well with your fave salad and pasta .

Any Holiday Veggie Casserole

It's a great recipe for any time of the year that's easy to cook and mouth-watering! You may add in your last night's left-over for instant dish.

Ingredients:

2 cups potatoes, cubed 1"
2 pieces large plump beefsteak tomatoes, quartered
½ cup red apples, minced
¼ cup chopped pineapple tidbits
¼ cup chopped raisins
1 cup chestnuts, roasted, shelled and finely chopped
¼ cup chopped cashew nuts
¼ cup chopped onions
¼ cup chopped carrots
¼ cup chopped celery
¼ cup cubed green bell pepper
2 pcs vegan sausage, finely chopped
¼ cup vegan ham, chopped finely
¼ cup chopped lef-over food
¼ cup grated Mozarella cheese
¼ tsp cinnamon powder
5 tablespoon olive oil
1 cup coconut milk
1 cup chicken broth
1 tbsp balsamic vinegar
½ cup brown sugar
½ cup maple syrup

Sprinkle with:

¼ teaspoon paprika
a dash of salt and pepper to taste for each

Directions:

Put all the cooking oil in a casserole over high heat. Mix in the onions, peppers, celery and carrots. Saute' for 3 minutes.

Add all the ingredients and stir once. Simmer for 15-20 minutes

Serving suggestion:

Transfer on big serving bowl. It goes well with your favorite fresh salad or rice risotto.

Veggie Meat With Figs Casserole

The sweet and aromatic figs add the zesty flavor to this vegan's delight recipe.

Ingredients:

2 cups veggie meat, cubed 2"
3 pcs firm tofu squares, deep fried and quartered
1 cup ripe figs, chopped finely
1 cup potatoes, peeled and cubed 2"
½ cup carrots, peeled and cubed 2"
1/2 cup cabbage leaves, sliced thinly
1 cup coconut water
¼ cup chopped garlic
¼ cup young onion bulbs
2 tablespoons corn oil
Flavor with:

1 tablespoon chopped chives
a dash of paprika
a dash of pepper to taste

Sauce:

2 cups coconut milk
2 tablespoons soya flour
½ cup brown sugar
½ cup maple syrup
1 tsp cane vinegar

Directions:

Heat the cooking oil in a casserole. Saute' the garlic, onions and veggies for 5 minutes. Stir in all the ingredients. Cover and simmer for 15 minutes in high heat.

Mix sauce ingredients with the coconut milk in a separate small casserole. Cover and simmer for 5 minutes in high heat, until sauce thickens.

Transfer the mouthwatering stew in a hot sizzling plate. Pour the thickened sauce.

Serving suggestion:

Pesto Lasagna With Pine Nuts And Penne

It's a healthy and budget-friendly dish that can be concocted any time of the day.

Ingredients:

Pesto Mixture:

2 cups fresh basil leaves, finely chopped
¼ cup fresh oregano leaves, finely chopped
1 cup fresh spinach leaves, finely chopped
1 cup cucumbers, seeded and cubed
2 cups pine nuts, chopped
1 cup chopped garlic
2 medium white onions, finely chopped
a teaspoon of salt and pepper
a teaspoon of white vinegar
a teaspoon of brown sugar or molasses

Cheese mixture:

2 cups Edam cheese, shaved
2 cups Brie cheese, minced
2 cups Mozzarella cheese, minced
½ cup cornstarch
½ cup water
¼ tablespoon dried rosemary
1 teaspoon garlic, minced
¼ tsp. star anise seed, powdered

¼ teaspoon dried basil
¼ teaspoon seasalt
3 large vegan eggs

Pasta:

1 pound Lasagna noodles
2 cups Penne noodles
2 tbsp olive oil
5-7 cups water
2 tbsp rock salt

Toppings:

3-5 tbsp. grated cheese of your choice

Directions:

Boil the lasagna and penne noodles for 10 minutes with water and oil until "al dente" or firm when touched or cut with fingers. It should not be mushy. Prepare the mixture and sauces while cooking the pasta.

Place all the vegetables and pesto mixture in a food processor and pulse for 30 seconds. Set aside and cover.

Place the all the cheese with herbs, garlic salt, spices, flour, water and beaten eggs in a small saucepan and stir. Simmer for 5 minutes and until sauce thickens

Brush a tablespoon of cooking oil at the bottom of the casserole and placed one layer of cooked lasagna and penne. Pour a cup of pesto sauce at the bottom of the casserole.

Put a layer of noodles on top of the sauce, covering the entire surface. You may cut the pasta to fit the casserole.

Layer half of the cheese mixture on top of the pasta, and then pour 1 cup of the pesto sauce and one cup of cheese mixture on top.

Repeat with another layer of noodles, followed by the remaining cheese and vegetable mixture.

Pour the remaining pasta sauce on top of the lasagna and top with the remaining cup of the grated cheese. Sprinkle a dash of salt and pepper.

Bake at 350° in a casserole for 1 hour or until cheese melted and sauce is bubbling hot.

Topped the pasta with pine nuts and grated cheese.

Serving suggestion:

Serve hot with onion soup, fresh green salad and roti bread.

Vietnamese Rolls With Special Vegan Sauce

It's a healthy and budget-friendly cuisine that can be prepared any time of the day.

Ingredients:

8-10 thin and transparent or flour wraps
8-10 chives leaves, for tying rolls

Roll Mixture:

1 cup fresh watercress leaves, blanched and finely chopped
1 cup fresh spinach leaves, blanched and finely chopped
½ cup white radish, finely chopped
½ cup cucumbers, seeded and julienned
1 cup peanuts, chopped
¼ cup chopped garlic
1 medium white onions, finely chopped
a teaspoon of salt and pepper
a teaspoon of lime juice
a teaspoon of brown sugar

Special sauce:

2 tbsp peanut oil
1 tbsp annatto seed oil
1 tbsp sesame oil
2 tbsp cornstarch

2 cups water
2 tbsp molasses or brown sugar
1 cup peanut butter

Toppings:

2 tbsp. roasted sesame seeds
3 tbsp. sesame oil for drizzling
3 tbsp. honey for drizzling

Directions:

Put the sauce ingredients in a small saucepan and simmer for 5 minutes. Stir until sauce thickens. Set aside and cover.

Place all the vegetables and roll mixture in a small bowl and combine with clean hands. Set aside and cover.

Put a tablespoon of veggie mixture into the wraps and roll up. Tie with chives leaves to secure ends.

Brush a tablespoon of cooking oil at the bottom of the casserole and place one by one the rolls. Pour the special sauce over the rolls. Cover the casserole and simmer for 3 minutes.

Transfer to serving platter and top with roasted sesame seeds. Drizzle with sesame oil and honey.

Serving suggestion:

Serve immediately with your favorite steamed risotto or fresh fruit salad.

Spicy Lettuce Rolls With Fruity Stew

It's a healthy and budget-friendly veggie rolls that can be prepared any time of the day and can be enjoyed by non-vegans

Ingredients:

8-10 fresh lettuce leaves, washed and drained
8-10 chives leaves, for tying rolls

Roll Mixture:

1 cup fresh unripe saba (Cardaba) bananas, finely chopped
1 cup pineapple tidbits, finely chopped
1 cup fresh baby squash leaves, finely chopped
½ cup white turnips, peeled and julienned
½ cup bean sprouts, washed and drained
1 pc. Brussel sprouts, chopped
1 cup peanuts, chopped
3 tbsp vegetable oil
¼ cup chopped garlic
1 medium red onions, finely chopped
a teaspoon of cayenne powder
a teaspoon of salt and pepper
a teaspoon of lemon juice
a teaspoon of brown sugar

Special sauce:

2 tbsp peanut oil
1 tbsp sesame oil
3 tbsp cornstarch
1 cup pineapple juice
2 cups water
3 tbsp molasses or brown sugar
1 cup peanut butter
a teaspoon of lemon juice
a teaspoon of grated horseradish
2 cups squash, peeled and pureed

Toppings:

2 tbsp. roasted chilli red peppers, chopped
2 tbsp. roasted sesame seeds
3 tbsp. maple syrup for drizzling

Directions:

Put the sauce ingredients in a small saucepan and simmer for 5 minutes. Stir until sauce thickens. Set aside and cover.

In a casserole, sauté onions, brussel sprouts and garlic with oil until soft. Add in all the vegetables and fruits with the other ingredients. Simmer for 3 minutes. Set aside and cool slightly.

Place the lettuce leaves on a flat surface. Put a tablespoon of roll mixture into the leaves and roll up. Tie with chives leaves to secure ends.

Arrange and place one by one the rolls on a serving platter. Pour the special sauce over the rolls. Drizzle with sesame seeds, chopped chilis and maple syrup.

Serving suggestion:

Serve immediately with your favorite chicken barbeque and roasted red bell peppers.

Saba Burgers With Veggie Stew Sauce

Who would think that banana peels can be eaten? These budget-friendly cooking banana burgers are packed with vitamins and yummy too!

Ingredients:

Burger mixture:

2 cups fresh unripe saba (Cardaba) bananas, finely chopped
1 cup saba peels, boiled and finely chopped
1 cup pineapple tidbits, finely chopped
1 cup fresh carrots, finely chopped
1 cup fresh turnips, finely chopped
1 pc. red bell pepper, finely chopped
1 tbsp vegetable oil
¼ cup chopped garlic
1 large red onions, finely chopped
¼ cup chopped celery stick
a teaspoon of salt and pepper
a teaspoon of calamansi juice
a teaspoon of brown sugar
3 large eggs, beaten
3 tbsp cornstarch
½ cup corn oil, for frying the burgers

Special sauce:

2 tbsp corn oil

5 tbsp cornstarch
¼ cup finely chopped beets
½ cup pineapple juice
½ cup soy sauce
½ cup water
3 tbsp brown sugar
1 cup truffle cream
a teaspoon of grated nutmeg
a dash of cinnamon

Directions:

Put the sauce ingredients in a small casserole and simmer for 10 minutes. Stir until sauce thickens. Set aside and cover.

Combine all the burger mixture until well-mixed. Form into golf-size balls. Fry and flatten as you would hamburger patties until crispy brown.

Arrange and place one by one the saba burgers on a serving platter. Pour the special sauce over the rolls. You may drizzle it with maple syrup and chopped chives.

Serving suggestion:

5 Ingredients Or Less Vegetarian Recipes

Almond Broccoli Salad

Ingredients:

3-4 broccoli florets, chopped
One cup of almond slices, toasted
Salt and pepper to taste
One cup of olive oil/vinegar (any variety) mix

Directions:

Boil florets in a medium saucepan for three minutes. Drain immediately and place inside large mixing bowl.

Mix in oil/vinegar mix and let sit for five minutes before adding almonds and seasoning.

Refrigerate for one hour before serving.

Apple Celery Salad

On a lazy summer afternoon, apple celery salad makes a really cool option to eat for freshnening you up. It is easy to make and tasty to eat.

Ingredients:

2 cups of Granny Smith apples, peeled and cubed
A large bunch of celery leaves
2 tablespoons of lemon juice
½ cup of honey
¾ cup of walnuts, chopped

Directions:

Peel the apples and take out the seeds. Cut the apple into wedges and then further into small triangular cubes. Roughly chop the celery leaves.
In a medium sized bowl add in the apples, celery, honey and lemon juice. Toss them all together. In the end, add in the chopped walnuts for an extra crunch and toss again.

Serve immediately.

Apple Pear Salad

During the scorching summer heat, an apple and pear salad makes a great meal. It is something which your whole family can not only enjoy as a side dish, but as a main course as well.

Ingredients:

1 cup of firm pears, cut into chunks
1 cup of tart apples, cut into chunks
A pinch of salt and pepper each
Juice of 1 lemon
1 teaspoon of sugar

Directions:

Wash and cut the apples and the pears into the chunks of same size. In a medium sized serving bowl, add in the apples and the pears. Sprinkles some salt and pepper and add in the sugar. In the end, squeeze some fresh lemon juice on the top and toss all the ingredients.

Serve chilled.

Serving Suggestions:

You can also make your own variations in the salad by adding cream, chopped walnuts and even Boston lettuce.

Asian Lettuce Wraps

Asian lettuce wraps are full of flavor because of the different sauces used in them. You can make a simple lettuce wrap for yourself or you can put in more ingredients of your choice, all depending upon the availability of time.

Ingredients:

Romaine lettuce hearts, as needed
2 ears of corn
2 tablespoons of Soy sauce
1 tablespoon of Chili powder, or as per your taste
2 teaspoons of Peanut oil

Directions:

Take a non-stick frying pan and heat the Peanut oil in it. If you are using fresh corns then make sure that you have already taken them off from the cobs.

Cook the corns in the oil for a few minutes. Make sure that the corns don't lose their crunchiness. Add in the chili powder and Soy sauce and cook until the corns have almost dried up.

Spoon out the mixture onto the lettuce leaves, fold and start munching.

Avocado Dip

Avocado dip makes a nice side dish with any grilled vegetables. It is a bit tangy and extremely yummy.

Ingredients:

1 ½ cups of ripe Avocados, roughly chopped
½ cup of tomatoes, seeds removed
1 clove of garlic, crushed
Juice of 1 lemon

Directions:

Chop the avocados into small chunks and deseed the tomatoes.

Take a blender and throw all the ingredients in it. Buzz until all the ingredients are well combined. Serve with grilled vegetables or fried potatoes.

Serving Suggestions:

You can also add Greek yogurt into the dip as well.

Baked Bean Soup

Baked bean soup makes a cold winter Sunday, a cozy one. the flavor of beans combined with any vegetables of your choice provides comfort and fills your appetite.

Ingredients:

½ cup of chopped onion
16 oz can of baked beans
5 cups of vegetable stock and tomato puree mixture
Paprika, as per taste
Worcestershire Sauce, as needed

Directions:

Take a large pot and sauté the chopped onion until it turns a light golden brown. Add in the can of baked beans and sauté them as well for a few minutes. Add in the Worcestershire sauce and season with paprika.
Pour in the vegetable stock and tomato puree mixture and mix all the ingredients with the help of a large cooking spoon.
Bring the mixture to a boil and turn down the flame to low. Let the soup simmer on a low flame for at least 15 minutes, or until all the ingredients are well incorporated into each other.

Serving Suggestions:
Serve hot with garlic bread.

Baked Eggplant Sandwiches

It is the game night and you are craving for something as exciting as the tournament is! Then these baked eggplant sandwiches will make your night even more fun.

Ingredients:

1 lb long eggplant (1 medium almost)
¾ cup of Parmesan cheese, finely grated
1 small jar of sun dried tomatoes, in oil
¾ cup of breadcrumbs
3 eggs

Directions:

Cut the eggplant into thin slices no more than ¼ inches in size. Sprinkle some salt onto the eggplants. Set aside for 30 minutes. After 30 minutes, rinse the eggplants and pat them dry with a paper towel.
Preheat your oven to 375 degrees and grease a baking dish with cooking spray.
Drain all the excess oil from the sundried tomatoes and start assembling the sandwiches.
Place one egg plant onto a flat surface and sprinkle some Parmesan on the top. Cover with a sun dried tomato and again sprinkle more cheese. Sprinkle some seasoning on the top and in the end, place another slice of eggplant for completing your sandwich.

Repeat the same process with the other eggplants. Slightly beat the eggs and dip each eggplant sandwich into the eggs and then coat in the bread crumbs. Bake in a preheated oven for 30 to 40 minutes or until the bread crumbs turn a nice golden brown. Make sure to turn the eggplants through half of the cooking time.

Serving Suggestions:

Serve hot with gherkins and your favorite dip.

Baked Mac And Cheese

Mac and Cheese is an all-time favorite of almost every household in America. The best thing about making it is that you don't have to use any type of fancy ingredients in making it, and it always comes out as extremely yummy.

Directions:
1 package of Macaroni
2 cups of Milk
2 tablespoons of melted Butter
2 ½ cups of grated cheddar cheese
Salt and Pepper, according to taste
Ingredients:

Preheat your oven to 375 degrees. Grease a 12 inch casserole dish sparingly, with cooking spray.
Add water and salt in a medium sized pot and bring the water to a boil. Add in the macaroni and cook them until they are half done.
In a medium sized bowl mix together the milk, butter and cheese. Add in the salt and pepper and mix well.
Put the macaroni in the casserole dish and pour the milk and cheese mixture over it. Mix the macaroni with the mixture.
Bake in a preheated oven for 30 minutes or until the cheese melts and the top becomes a nice golden brown.

Bean Burritos

Bean burritos make a very interesting food during the meal time. Eat them as It is, or with a dip, they are heavenly!

Ingredients:

A 16 oz can of refried beans
1 cup of long grain rice, cooked
1 cup of salsa
2 cups of cheddar cheese, divided
12 flour tortillas

Directions:

Preheat your oven to 375 degrees and coat your baking tray generously with cooking spray.
In a medium sized bowl mix together the beans, salsa and half of the cheddar cheese. With the help of the spoon, divide the mixture equally on the tortillas and fold their sides. Finally roll the tortillas.
Place the tortillas on the baking dish and bake in a preheated oven for at least 15 minutes. A well cooked burrito is evenly heated through.

Cranberry Crumble

Cranberry crumble is an ideal dessert for any occasion. Be it any party at your kid's school or a tea party at your place, cranberry crumble is easy to make and delicious to eat.

Ingredients:

1 package of fresh cranberries
¾ cup of brown sugar
1 ½ cups of all-purpose flour
1 ½ cups of quick cooking oatmeal
¾ cup of butter, melted

Directions:

Preheat oven to 375 degrees and grease a 9x9 inches oven proof pan with cooking spray.

First of all, prepare the cranberries according to the Directions written on the packet. You can also use canned cranberries, is you can't get hold of the fresh ones.
Mix all the ingredients, except the pats, into the prepared cranberries mixture.
For assembling the crumble, place the oatmeal onto the pan while pressing evenly with your hands. Top

with the cranberries mixture. In the end sprinkle the remaining oatmeal on the top.

Bake in a preheated oven for almost 30 minutes or when the top starts getting a nice light golden brown.

Chorizo Beans

Ingredients:

One cup of white beans, cooked
One cup (or ½ link) of soy chorizo
One small onion, chopped small
½ cup of salsa (any variety)

Directions:

In a large pan, heat chorizo on medium heat.

Mix in by beans and onions and cover. Let mixture cook for five minutes.

Stir in salsa and remove from heat.

Let sit for 10 minutes before serving with tortillas.

Easy Chimis

Ingredients:

One can of refried beans (vegetarian)
One cup of pico de gallo or chunky salsa
One baked potato, chopped small
6 medium tortillas
One cup of vegetable of canola oil

Directions:

Using a large skillet, start to heat oil on low. In a large bowl, mix beans, salsa and potato until even.

Place two heaping teaspoons near the edge of tortilla. Fold ends inward, and then roll horizontally. Place inside oil immediately to secure.

Cook for 7-10 minutes on each side and drain on paper towel. Serve with sour cream or Ranch, if desired.

Easy Pot Pie

Ingredients:

One bag of frozen vegetables (any variety)
One can of mushroom soup, creamed
Two tablespoons of all-purpose seasoning
One tablespoon of ground pepper
One frozen pie crust, double

Directions:

Preheat oven to 350 degrees and prepare pie bottom as directed. In a medium bowl, mix remaining ingredients until even.

When pie bottom has finished baking, add mixture followed by pie top. Cook for 25-35 minutes and brush top with one beaten egg or melted butter for browning.

Cook for an additional 10 minutes and let cool for five minutes before serving.

Famous Cabbage Soup

Ingredients:

One head of cabbage, shredded
One can of tomatoes, chopped
One large carrot, chopped small
One large onion, chopped small
Salt and pepper to taste

Directions:

Boil carrots in 3 cups of water, followed by onions and cabbage. Cover and remove from heat for about 10 minutes.

Let simmer for about 20 minutes after stirring in tomatoes and seasonings.

Eat as part of a weight management program that calls for non-starchy vegetables.

Garlic Brussels Sprouts

Ingredients:

10-12 Brussels sprouts, halved
Two teaspoons of crushed garlic
One teaspoon of honey or agave nectar
Two teaspoon of olive or vegetable oil
Salt and pepper to taste

Directions:

In a large skillet, heat oil on medium, followed by sprouts. Cover and let cook for five minutes, or until slightly soft.

Reduce heat and add garlic, sweetener and seasonings.

Cover and remove from heat. Let sit for at least five minutes before serving.

Green Bean And Lentil Stew

Green bean and lentil stew is a perfect combination of different types of proteins together. A perfect treat on a cold winter day for soothing your nerves and fulfilling your appetite.

Ingredients:

¾ cup of brown lentils, rinsed and dried
1 cup of green beans, sliced
3 sun dried tomatoes, finely chopped
½ teaspoon of thyme leaves
2 tablespoons of extra virgin olive oil

Directions:

Heat the olive oil in a pan and add the lentils in it. Sauté for a few minutes and then add in the tomatoes. Cook for a few minutes, while stirring them occasionally. Add in enough water to cook the lentils in, almost 2 cups, and bring the water to a boil.
Turn down the flame to low, and let the lentils simmer for at least 40 minutes or until the lentils have become really soft. You can keep on adding more water, if required.
Add in the green beans and give them all a stir. Let the green beans simmer with the lentils until the green beans are fully cooked. It will hardly take 15 minutes. Season with salt.

Serving Suggestions:

Serve with any bread of your choice or as it is.

Grilled Cheese And Peppers On Sour Dough

BBQ nights don't always have to involve meat. You can have a fun filled BBQ night with grilled cheese and peppers on Sourdough.

Ingredients:

4 slices of Sourdough
4 slices of pepper jack cheese
2 slices of tomato
¼ cup of fresh basil leaves, chopped
Butter, as needed

Directions:

Turn on your grill and start assembling the sandwiches. On your work surface, place a slice of bread and top it with a slice of cheese. Put a tomato slice on the top and sprinkle some basil leaves. Place another cheese slice and again another slice of bread.
With the help of a brush coat the grill pan with butter and start grilling the sandwiches on one side. When the side starts turning brown and the cheese starts to melt, flip the sandwich and grill again.

Serving Suggestions:
Serve with your favorite salad.

Lemon Basil Pasta

This light lemon basil pasta makes a great lunch and dinner time option. A great treat to enjoy with your friends and family during summer time.

Ingredients:

1 (10 oz) package of pasta, any of your choice
1 can of cannellini beans, drained
Zest of ½ a lemon
1 cup of fresh basil leaves
2 ½ tablespoons of olive oil

Directions:

Cook the pasta according to the Directions written on the packet. When the pasta is almost cooked, add in the beans. Drain with the help of a colander.
Heat the olive oil in a pan and add the lemon zest in it. Sauté for just about 30 seconds. Put the sautéed zest along with the olive oil in a food processor. Add in the basil leaves, juice from the same lemon, and the seasoning. Keep on adding water until the consistency you required is reached.
Add the pasta into a bowl and pour the lemon and basil mixture over it. Toss and serve hot.

Lentil Soup

The traditional lentils soup is made with a variety of ingredients. You can add not only lentils in it but also any vegetables of your choice as well. but a simple lentils soup can be really yummy as well and you can actually relish the taste of lentils in it.

Ingredients:

1 lb of lentils, any of your choice
2 cups of vegetable broth
2 tablespoons of olive oil
½ teaspoon of freshly ground cumin seeds
½ teaspoon of freshly ground coriander seeds

Directions:

Clean the lentils and rinse them with water.
Take a medium sized pot and add the olive oil in it. Sauté the lentils until they change their color slightly.
Add in the vegetable stock and stir the lentils. Bring the stock to a boil and add in the seasoning, ground cumin seeds and coriander seeds.
Turn th flame to medium low and let the soup simmer until the lentils are properly cooked.
Puree the soup with the help of a stick blender. Serve warm.

Part 2

Introduction

For many people, side dishes play just a minor role in a meal. However, they're good for your health as long as you pick the right side dishes. Since their ingredients are mostly fruits and veggies, they have fewer calories than main dishes do. Side dishes help prevent many health problems, including cancers and heart disease.
Making yummy side-dishes will take you just a few minutes. Save more time by preparing a side dish while you're cooking the main dish.

Don't worry if the veggies in your fridge go to bed. Simply follow our side-dish casserole recipes to come up with great dishes everyone will love.

Keep In Touch.

You also see more different types of side dish recipes such as:

- Sauces & Condiments
- Side Dish for Two
- Thanksgiving Side Dishes
- Diabetic Side Dishes
- Italian Side Dish
- ...

Let's live happily and cook yourself every day!
Enjoy the book,

Mcdonalds Fries

"McDonald's fries are the best. Just how you love them."

Serving: 4 | Prep: 10 m | Cook: 10 m | Ready in: 1 h 15 m

Ingredients

- 8 potatoes, peeled and cut into 1/4-inch thick fries
- 1/4 cup white sugar
- 2 tablespoons corn syrup
- 1 quart canola oil, or as needed
- sea salt to taste

Direction

- Place potatoes in a bowl and cover with water; let sit for 5 minutes. Drain and pat dry.
- Place potatoes in a bowl and cover with boiling water; add sugar and corn syrup and mix well. Place bowl in the refrigerator and let sit for 5 minutes. Drain and pat dry.
- Spread potatoes out in a baking dish, cover the dish with plastic wrap, and freeze for 30 minutes.
- Heat oil in a deep-fryer or large saucepan to 350 degrees F (175 degrees C).
- Working in batches, fry potatoes in hot oil for 2 minutes. Transfer to a paper towel-lined plate to dry and let cool for 15 minutes.

- Working in batches again, fry potatoes in hot oil until browned and crispy, 5 to 7 minutes. Season fries with sea salt.

Nutrition Information

- Calories: 600 calories
- Total Fat: 22.4 g
- Cholesterol: 0 mg
- Sodium: 112 mg
- Total Carbohydrate: 94.8 g
- Protein: 8.6 g

Mexican Style Corn

"On the streets of Santa Maria, California, street vendors (think an ice cream man with a 'trash can' full of hot corn on the cob instead of ice cream) roam the sidewalks selling corn on the cob for a dollar an ear! They slide a wooden skewer in one end for you to hold the corn. We crave it often and it's become a regular on our Saturday grill nights! Give it a try. You'll be surprised!"

Serving: 4 | Prep: 15 m | Cook: 20 m | Ready in: 35 m
Ingredients

- 4 ears corn on the cob, husks and silk removed
- 1/4 cup mayonnaise (such as Hellmann's®/Best Foods®), or to taste - divided
- 1/4 cup margarine in a squeezable container, or to taste - divided
- 1/4 cup grated Parmesan cheese, or to taste - divided
- 1 teaspoon chili powder, or to taste - divided

Direction

- Bring a large pot of water to a boil and gently place ears of corn into the boiling water. Reduce heat to low and simmer until corn is very tender, 20 to 25 minutes.
- Remove an ear of corn with tongs and spread about 1 tablespoon of mayonnaise all over the kernels.

Squeeze about 1 tablespoon of margarine over the ear of corn in a zig-zag line, turning the ear as you squeeze. Generously sprinkle Parmesan cheese over the ear and dust with chili powder. Repeat with remaining ears of corn.

Nutrition Information

- Calories: 300 calories
- Total Fat: 24.7 g
- Cholesterol: 10 mg
- Sodium: 306 mg
- Total Carbohydrate: 18.2 g
- Protein: 5.2 g

Microwave Cornonthecob In The Husk

"This is one of my favorite ways to fix corn on the cob, even when I have several to fix. Without the water from boiling, the corn stays nice and sweet. Hope this helps just one young cook."

Serving: 1 | Prep: 5 m | Cook: 5 m | Ready in: 10 m

Ingredients

- 1 ear fresh corn in the husk

Direction

- Rinse entire ear of corn under water briefly. Wrap corn in a paper towel and place on a microwave-safe plate.
- Cook corn in the microwave oven until hot and cooked through, 3 to 5 minutes. Remove from microwave and let rest for 2 minutes. Remove corn husk.

Nutrition Information

- Calories: 77 calories
- Total Fat: 1.1 g
- Cholesterol: 0 mg
- Sodium: 14 mg
- Total Carbohydrate: 17.1 g
- Protein: 2.9 g

Mouthwatering Brown Sugar Bacon

"My grandpa was the biggest bacon lover I know... and this was his favorite bacon recipe! The brown sugar caramelizes onto the bacon, making a mouthwatering sweet and savory treat!"

Serving: 6 | Prep: 10 m | Cook: 10 m | Ready in: 20 m
Ingredients

- 1 pound thick-sliced bacon
- 1/2 cup brown sugar
- 1/4 cup chopped pecans (optional)

Direction

- Preheat the oven to 350 degrees F (175 degrees C). Line a baking sheet with aluminum foil.
- Arrange bacon on the baking sheet in a single layer; edges can touch or slightly overlap. Sprinkle brown sugar generously on top. Sprinkle pecans over the sugar.
- Bake in the preheated oven until browned and glazed, 10 to 15 minutes.

Nutrition Information

- Calories: 239 calories
- Total Fat: 13.9 g
- Cholesterol: 27 mg
- Sodium: 579 mg
- Total Carbohydrate: 19.1 g

- Protein: 9.7 g

My Muminlaws Lightly Fried Plantains

"My mother-in-law, Sathiabama Sriharan, came from London to the Upper East Side of New York City to help me take care of my first child when she was 2.5 months old. Not only did she teach me about what to expect each week in raising a growing baby, she helped me shed the baby weight and eat healthy as a nursing mother by preparing healthy, quick, and easy meals. Hope you try it and like it. Enjoy and bon appetite!"

Serving: 4 | Prep: 10 m | Cook: 10 m | Ready in: 20 m
Ingredients

- 2 tablespoons olive oil
- 2 large plantains, peeled and sliced into 1-inch pieces
- 2 teaspoons sour cream, or to taste (optional)

Direction

- Heat olive oil in a skillet over medium heat; arrange half the plantain pieces, without overlapping, in the hot oil. Cook until lightly browned, about 2 minutes per side; drain plantains on a paper towel-lined plate. Repeat with remaining plantain pieces. Serve hot with sour cream.

Nutrition Information

- Calories: 233 calories
- Total Fat: 7.8 g
- Cholesterol: 1 mg
- Sodium: 7 mg
- Total Carbohydrate: 44 g
- Protein: 1.9 g

Nancys Butter Beans

"Butter beans with bacon are delicious."

Serving: 2 | Prep: 10 m | Cook: 15 m | Ready in: 25 m

Ingredients

- 2 slices bacon
- 1 (15 ounce) can butter beans, rinsed and drained
- 1 tablespoon butter
- 1 tablespoon brown sugar
- salt and ground black pepper to taste

Direction

- Arrange bacon in a large skillet and cook over medium-high heat, turning occasionally, until evenly browned, about 10 minutes. Drain on paper towels and crumble.
- Heat butter beans, bacon, butter, and brown sugar in a saucepan over medium heat until bubbling, about 5 minutes. Season with salt and pepper.

Nutrition Information

- Calories: 274 calories
- Total Fat: 9.5 g
- Cholesterol: 25 mg
- Sodium: 995 mg
- Total Carbohydrate: 33.2 g
- Protein: 13.3 g

No Cook Applesauce

"Yummy applesauce for the whole family. This serving size is for a crowd so you might want to make it smaller. Everyone will love it."

Serving: 16 | Prep: 15 m | Ready in: 15 m
Ingredients

- 12 apples - peeled, cored, and chopped
- 1 cup brown sugar
- 1 cup water
- 1 1/2 tablespoons lemon juice
- 1 teaspoon ground cinnamon

Direction

- Blend apples, brown sugar, water, lemon juice, and cinnamon in a blender until smooth.

Nutrition Information

- Calories: 107 calories
- Total Fat: 0.2 g
- Cholesterol: 0 mg
- Sodium: 5 mg
- Total Carbohydrate: 28 g
- Protein: 0.3 g

Nutmeg Mashed Potatoes

"The perfect fall side dish for any steak and made with real potatoes: festive nutmeg-flavored mashed potato."

Serving: 6 | Prep: 10 m | Cook: 20 m | Ready in: 30 m

Ingredients

- 4 large potatoes
- 1/4 cup butter
- 2 teaspoons ground nutmeg, or to taste
- 2 teaspoons salt, or to taste
- 1/2 cup sour cream

Direction

- Place potatoes into a large pot and cover with salted water; bring to a boil. Reduce heat to medium-low and simmer until potatoes are tender and split open, about 20 minutes. Drain and return potatoes to pot.
- Mash potatoes with butter, nutmeg, and salt using a potato masher or fork until well incorporated; stir in sour cream until mashed potatoes are creamy.

Nutrition Information

- Calories: 304 calories
- Total Fat: 12.3 g
- Cholesterol: 29 mg
- Sodium: 801 mg

- Total Carbohydrate: 44.3 g
- Protein: 5.7 g

Orange Wild Rice With Pistachios And Cranberries

"Dried cranberries and pistachios are added to wild rice that has a mild orange flavor to yield a hearty and easy side or main dish."

Serving: 4 | Prep: 10 m | Cook: 45 m | Ready in: 55 m
Ingredients

- 1 cup orange juice
- 1 cup wild rice
- 3/4 cup water
- 1/3 cup shelled pistachios
- 1/3 cup dried cranberries

Direction

- Combine orange juice, rice, and water in a saucepan; bring to a boil, reduce heat to low, cover saucepan with a lid, and simmer until rice is tender, about 45 minutes. Remove from heat and let steam, covered, for 10 minutes more. Stir pistachios and cranberries into rice.

Nutrition Information

- Calories: 259 calories
- Total Fat: 5.2 g
- Cholesterol: 0 mg

- Sodium: 48 mg
- Total Carbohydrate: 47.4 g
- Protein: 8.5 g

Oven Baked Parsley Red Potatoes

"This is a recipe that my grandmother made ever since I can remember (I'm 58). I bake the potatoes like she did and serve them with pork or chicken. It's a favorite of my father-in-law who always asks for them when he comes for dinner."

Serving: 8 | Prep: 10 m | Cook: 40 m | Ready in: 50 m
Ingredients

- 1/2 cup butter, cubed
- 2 pounds red potatoes, halved
- 1 tablespoon minced onion, or to taste
- 2 tablespoons minced fresh parsley
- 1/2 teaspoon salt
- 1/4 teaspoon ground black pepper

Direction

- Preheat oven to 375 degrees F (190 degrees C). Place butter in a large baking dish and melt in preheating oven.
- Toss potatoes and onion in melted butter to coat.
- Bake in preheated oven until potatoes are tender, about 40 minutes. Sprinkle parsley over potatoes and season with salt and pepper; toss.

Nutrition Information

- Calories: 182 calories
- Total Fat: 11.7 g
- Cholesterol: 31 mg
- Sodium: 234 mg
- Total Carbohydrate: 18.3 g
- Protein: 2.3 g

Oven Roasted Baked Potatoes

"Yummy potatoes that can help to fill out a meal for a table full of hungry teenagers. Potatoes can be cooked until just done or cooked to a crunchy skin. Great either way."

Serving: 6 | Prep: 10 m | Cook: 30 m | Ready in: 40 m
Ingredients

- 8 fingerling potatoes, cubed
- 1 large onion, cubed
- 2 tablespoons coconut oil, melted
- 2 tablespoons minced garlic
- 1 tablespoon sea salt

Direction

- Preheat oven to 350 degrees F (175 degrees C). Line a large baking sheet with foil.
- Toss fingerling potatoes, onion, coconut oil, garlic, and sea salt in a large bowl. Spread mixture onto

baking sheet; bake, stirring every 10 minutes, until potatoes are tender, about 30 to 40 minutes.

Nutrition Information

- Calories: 149 calories
- Total Fat: 4.8 g
- Cholesterol: 0 mg
- Sodium: 889 mg
- Total Carbohydrate: 24.7 g
- Protein: 2.9 g

Ovenbaked Potato Fries

"This is a great recipe to get kids started learning how to cook. Take a day, take a week, teach them new things each day. We used this for our 'at-home' camp week. Taught the kids how to cook one new thing each day for an entire week."

Serving: 4 | Prep: 10 m | Cook: 30 m | Ready in: 40 m

Ingredients

- 2 pounds baking potatoes, each cut into six wedges
- 2 tablespoons olive oil
- 1/2 teaspoon dried thyme leaves
- 1/4 teaspoon ground black pepper
- salt to taste
- 1/4 cup shredded Cheddar cheese (optional)

Direction

- Preheat oven to 450 degrees F (230 degrees C).
- Arrange potato wedges on a baking sheet. Drizzle olive oil over the wedges; season with thyme, pepper, and salt. Turn wedges with a spatula to coat with oil and seasonings.
- Roast potato wedges for 15 minutes, turn, and continue roasting until soft in the center, about 15 minutes more. Transfer wedges to a platter and sprinkle cheese over them.

Nutrition Information

- Calories: 264 calories
- Total Fat: 9.3 g
- Cholesterol: 7 mg
- Sodium: 58 mg
- Total Carbohydrate: 39.9 g
- Protein: 6.4 g

Ovenroasted Broccolini

"Easy, yummy broccolini roasted in the oven."

Serving: 4 | Prep: 10 m | Cook: 10 m | Ready in: 20 m
Ingredients

- 2 bunches broccolini
- 3 teaspoons minced garlic
- 4 tablespoons olive oil
- salt and ground black pepper to taste
- 2 tablespoons grated Parmesan cheese, or to taste

Direction

- Set an oven rack about 6 inches from the heat source and preheat the oven's broiler. Line a roasting pan with aluminum foil.
- Spread broccolini in an even layer in the roasting pan. Sprinkle garlic over broccolini. Drizzle olive oil over the top. Season with salt and pepper.

- Place under the broiler and cook, watching closely, until lightly browned and stalks are tender, 6 to 8 minutes. Serve sprinkled with Parmesan cheese.

Nutrition Information

- Calories: 227 calories
- Total Fat: 14.2 g
- Cholesterol: 2 mg
- Sodium: 144 mg
- Total Carbohydrate: 16.8 g
- Protein: 9.1 g

Paleo Cauliflower Rice

"This paleo recipe is so quick, easy, and delicious and really a great substitute for rice if you're trying to eat low-carb. Your whole family will love it!"

Serving: 4 | Prep: 10 m | Cook: 5 m | Ready in: 15 m

Ingredients

- 1 large head cauliflower, cut into large chunks
- 2 tablespoons extra-virgin olive oil
- salt and ground black pepper to taste

Direction

- Place cauliflower chunks in a food processor and pulse until broken down into rice-size pieces.

- Heat olive oil in a skillet over medium heat; add cauliflower 'rice', salt, and pepper. Cover skillet and cook until heated through, 3 to 5 minutes. Remove lid and fluff 'rice' with a fork.

Nutrition Information

- Calories: 113 calories
- Total Fat: 7 g
- Cholesterol: 0 mg
- Sodium: 63 mg
- Total Carbohydrate: 11.1 g
- Protein: 4.2 g

Paleo Yam Dish

"This scrumptious yam recipe will have you drooling for it every time."

Serving: 4 | Prep: 5 m | Cook: 18 m | Ready in: 23 m
Ingredients

- 2 yams, thinly sliced
- 1 tablespoon coconut oil
- 1 1/2 teaspoons ground cinnamon

Direction

- Bring a large pot of water to a boil; add yams. Cook until very soft, about 8 minutes. Drain; peel off skins.
- Heat coconut oil in a large skillet over medium heat. Add yams; cook and stir until browned, 5 to 10 minutes. Sprinkle cinnamon on top.

Nutrition Information

- Calories: 267 calories
- Total Fat: 3.8 g
- Cholesterol: 0 mg
- Sodium: 18 mg
- Total Carbohydrate: 56.5 g
- Protein: 3.1 g

Panfried Asparagus With Onions

"Everyone that I make this for absolutely loves it! The onions are a great flavor contrast to the asparagus. This vegetable dish pairs as a great side with everything...fish, meat, chicken, or pasta."

Serving: 4 | Prep: 10 m | Cook: 6 m | Ready in: 16 m

Ingredients

- 1 tablespoon butter
- 1 pound asparagus, trimmed
- 1 tablespoon butter
- 1/4 cup sliced onion
- 1 pinch onion salt, or to taste

Direction

- Melt 1 tablespoon butter in a large skillet over medium-high heat.
- Cook and stir asparagus in melted butter until bright green, but still firm, 3 to 4 minutes.
- Stir 1 tablespoon butter and onion into asparagus; sprinkle with onion salt.
- Cook and stir until onion is slightly browned and asparagus are tender, 3 to 5 minutes.

Nutrition Information

- Calories: 78 calories
- Total Fat: 5.9 g

- Cholesterol: 15 mg
- Sodium: 126 mg
- Total Carbohydrate: 5.4 g
- Protein: 2.7 g

Panfried Fennel

"This is an easy way to prepare fennel bulbs. Fennel tastes great pan-fried and you don't need a lot of seasoning as fennel has so much flavor on its own, which just intensifies while sauteeing."

Serving: 4 | Prep: 5 m | Cook: 20 m | Ready in: 25 m
Ingredients

- 2 pounds fennel bulbs, sliced, green tops reserved
- 3 tablespoons olive oil, or as needed
- salt to taste
- 1 pinch lemon pepper, or to taste

Direction

- Chop fennel greens and set aside.
- Heat 1 tablespoon oil in a nonstick pan over medium heat. Lay some fennel slices in a single layer in the pan; cook until nicely browned on both sides, about 5 minutes. Season with salt and lemon pepper. Remove from pan. Add another tablespoon oil and layer in the next batch of fennel slices and cook the same way. Repeat with remaining oil and fennel. Serve sprinkled with fennel greens.

Nutrition Information

- Calories: 160 calories
- Total Fat: 10.6 g
- Cholesterol: 0 mg
- Sodium: 215 mg
- Total Carbohydrate: 16.6 g
- Protein: 2.8 g

Parmesanroasted Tomatoes

"A delicious vegetable side dish that goes with pretty much anything."

Serving: 6 | Prep: 5 m | Cook: 20 m | Ready in: 25 m
Ingredients

- 6 small tomatoes, halved
- 1 tablespoon olive oil
- 1 pinch salt
- ground black pepper to taste
- 1/2 cup grated Parmesan cheese

Direction

- Preheat the oven to 400 degrees F (200 degrees C).
- Place tomatoes in a bowl and toss gently with olive oil and season with salt and pepper. Arrange on a baking sheet and top each tomato half with Parmesan cheese.

- Bake in the preheated oven until Parmesan cheese is melted and slightly browned, 15 to 20 minutes.

Nutrition Information

- Calories: 65 calories
- Total Fat: 4.3 g
- Cholesterol: 6 mg
- Sodium: 132 mg
- Total Carbohydrate: 3.9 g
- Protein: 3.4 g

Patacones De Colombia Fried Plantains

"These are fried plantains that have been smashed and fried a second time. It is essential you use very ripe plantains. This recipe is straight from my Colombian mother-in-law. Enjoy!"

Serving: 3 | Prep: 10 m | Cook: 10 m | Ready in: 20 m
Ingredients

- 1/2 cup oil for frying
- 1 ripe plantain, peeled and cut into 1-inch rounds
- 1 pinch salt

Direction

- Place a plate, upside-down, onto a work surface.
- Heat oil in a large skillet over medium heat. Fry plantain slices in the hot oil until slightly browned, 2 to 3 minutes per side. Transfer plantain slices using a slotted spoon onto the upside-down plate, reserving oil in the skillet. Place a second plate, right-side up, onto the plantains. Smash the plantain slices by gently pressing the top plate into the bottom plate.
- Place the smashed plantains in the hot oil and fry until browned, 2 to 3 minutes per side. Transfer fried plantains to a paper towel-lined plate and sprinkle salt over plantains.

Nutrition Information

- Calories: 105 calories
- Total Fat: 3.9 g
- Cholesterol: 0 mg
- Sodium: 54 mg
- Total Carbohydrate: 19 g
- Protein: 0.8 g

Pinto Beans Muy Facil

"Pinto beans muy facil (very easy). Put them in a slow cooker before you go to work and they should be ready that evening."

Serving: 8 | Prep: 15 m | Cook: 4 h | Ready in: 12 h 15 m

Ingredients

- 1 pound dried pinto beans
- 1 onion, chopped
- 1 clove garlic, minced
- 2 jalapeno peppers, chopped
- salt and ground black pepper to taste

Direction

- Place pinto beans into a large bowl and cover with several inches of water; soak at least 8 hours and up to 24 hours. Drain and rinse before using.
- Place soaked pinto beans, onion, garlic, and jalapeno peppers in a slow cooker; pour enough

water over mixture to cover with several inches. Cook on Medium-Low, 4 to 6 hours. Season with salt and black pepper.

Nutrition Information

- Calories: 194 calories
- Total Fat: 0.9 g
- Cholesterol: 0 mg
- Sodium: 2 mg
- Total Carbohydrate: 35.8 g
- Protein: 12 g

Pomegranate Glazed Carrots

"A great side dish! Healthy and fast. You can use baby carrots."

Serving: 4 | Prep: 10 m | Cook: 15 m | Ready in: 25 m
Ingredients

- 1 tablespoon butter
- 3 cups peeled, sliced carrots
- salt and ground black pepper to taste
- 1/4 cup orange juice
- 1/4 cup pomegranate juice

Direction

- Melt butter in a skillet over medium heat. Cook and stir carrots in the hot butter until they begin to soften, about 5 minutes; season with salt and black pepper.
- Stir orange juice and pomegranate juice into carrots, bring to a simmer, and reduce heat to low. Simmer carrots until tender, stirring occasionally, 10 to 12 minutes.

Nutrition Information

- Calories: 80 calories
- Total Fat: 3.1 g
- Cholesterol: 8 mg
- Sodium: 84 mg

- Total Carbohydrate: 12.9 g
- Protein: 1 g

Quick And Easy Baked Carrots

"Baked carrots with light sweet glaze."

Serving: 4 | Prep: 5 m | Cook: 20 m | Ready in: 25 m
Ingredients

- 1 bunch carrots, trimmed
- butter-flavored cooking spray (such as I Can't Believe It's Not Butter®)
- 1 teaspoon ground nutmeg
- 1 teaspoon ground cinnamon
- 1 teaspoon white sugar

Direction

- Preheat oven to 425 degrees F (220 degrees C).
- Arrange carrots in a shallow baking dish. Spray with cooking spray and sprinkle with nutmeg, cinnamon, and sugar.
- Bake in preheated oven until carrots are tender, 20 minutes.

Nutrition Information

- Calories: 68 calories
- Total Fat: 0.6 g
- Cholesterol: 0 mg
- Sodium: 101 mg
- Total Carbohydrate: 15.7 g
- Protein: 1.4 g

Quick And Easy Grilled Potatoes

"These are like a baked potato, but better! This recipe is so simple and makes a delicious side dish, a 'baked' potato that is soft in the middle and perfectly grilled on the outside. We dip ours in sour cream and green onions!"

Serving: 4 | Prep: 5 m | Cook: 22 m | Ready in: 27 m
Ingredients

- 2 large russet potatoes, scrubbed
- 2 tablespoons olive oil
- salt and ground black pepper to taste

Direction

- Poke each potato with the tines of a fork. Place the potatoes in a microwave oven, and cook on high power for about 5 minutes. Check about halfway through, and turn potatoes over for even cooking. Slice each potato in half the long way and cook potatoes another 2 minutes on high power.
- Preheat a grill for medium heat.
- Brush the potato tops with olive oil, and season with salt and pepper to taste.
- Cook on prepared grill for 15 to 20 minutes, turning once.

Nutrition Information

- Calories: 203 calories

- Total Fat: 6.9 g
- Cholesterol: 0 mg
- Sodium: 11 mg
- Total Carbohydrate: 32.2 g
- Protein: 3.7 g

Quick And Easy Mashed Sweet Potatoes

"This is my favorite quick and easy recipe. For more flavor, add maple syrup."

Serving: 4 | Prep: 10 m | Cook: 20 m | Ready in: 30 m

Ingredients

- 6 sweet potatoes
- 1/2 cup butter
- 2 cloves garlic, minced
- 1 teaspoon dried basil
- 1/2 teaspoon dried thyme

Direction

- Place potatoes into a large pot and cover with salted water; bring to a boil. Reduce heat to medium-low and simmer until tender, about 20 minutes; drain.
- Transfer potatoes to a large bowl; mash butter, garlic, basil, and thyme into the potatoes with a potato masher until smooth.

Nutrition Information

- Calories: 573 calories
- Total Fat: 23.3 g
- Cholesterol: 61 mg
- Sodium: 398 mg
- Total Carbohydrate: 86.6 g
- Protein: 7.1 g

Quick And Easy Panroasted Brussels Sprouts With Gorgonzola Cheese

"Savory Brussels sprouts all dressed up! This recipe calls for very few ingredients but creates a punch of flavor you're sure to love. This side pairs great with beef or lamb and a nice red wine."

Serving: 4 | Prep: 5 m | Cook: 11 m | Ready in: 16 m

Ingredients

- 2 tablespoons butter
- 1 (12 ounce) package fresh Brussels sprouts, halved
- 1/3 cup crumbled Gorgonzola cheese
- salt
- 1/4 teaspoon ground black pepper

Direction

- Heat a large skillet over medium-heat and melt butter. Add Brussels sprouts, turning to coat with butter. Cover skillet, reduce heat to medium, and cook, turning every 3 to 4 minutes, until Brussels sprouts are browned and tender, 8 to 10 minutes. Sprinkle with Gorgonzola cheese, salt, and pepper.

Nutrition Information

- Calories: 138 calories
- Total Fat: 10 g
- Cholesterol: 30 mg

- Sodium: 348 mg
- Total Carbohydrate: 7.7 g
- Protein: 5.9 g

Quick And Easy Parmesan Zucchini Fries

"Zucchinis, Parmesan cheese, garlic, and paprika make these ultimate zucchini fries, that are so easy to make, and carb-conscious as well!"

Serving: 4 | Prep: 15 m | Cook: 30 m | Ready in: 45 m
Ingredients

- cooking spray
- 2 eggs
- 3/4 cup grated Parmesan cheese
- 1 tablespoon dried mixed herbs
- 1 1/2 teaspoons garlic powder
- 1 teaspoon paprika
- 1/2 teaspoon ground black pepper
- 2 pounds zucchinis, cut into 1/2-inch French fry strips

Direction

- Preheat oven to 425 degrees F (220 degrees C). Line a baking sheet with aluminum foil and spray with cooking spray.

- Whisk eggs in a shallow bowl. Combine Parmesan cheese, mixed herbs, garlic powder, paprika, and pepper in a separate shallow bowl; mix well.
- Dip zucchini fries into beaten eggs, in batches; shake to remove excess, and roll in Parmesan mixture until fully coated. Place on the prepared baking sheet.
- Bake in the preheated oven, turning once, until golden and crispy, 30 to 35 minutes.

Nutrition Information

- Calories: 142 calories
- Total Fat: 7.2 g
- Cholesterol: 95 mg
- Sodium: 284 mg
- Total Carbohydrate: 10.4 g
- Protein: 11.7 g

Quick And Spicy Spaghetti Squash

"This one is good, try it!"

Serving: 4 | Prep: 10 m | Cook: 30 m | Ready in: 50 m
Ingredients

- 1 spaghetti squash, halved and seeded
- 2 tablespoons olive oil, divided
- 2 tablespoons chopped fresh parsley
- 1 tablespoon red pepper flakes
- salt and ground black pepper to taste

Direction

- Preheat oven to 350 degrees F (175 degrees C).
- Coat the inside of squash with about 1 tablespoon olive oil. Place squash, cut-side down, on a baking sheet.
- Bake in the preheated oven until squash is tender, about 30 minutes. Cool squash for 10 minutes.
- Shred the inside of squash with a fork and transfer to a bowl. Add remaining olive oil, parsley, red pepper flakes, salt, and pepper to shredded squash and toss to coat.

Nutrition Information

- Calories: 122 calories
- Total Fat: 8.2 g
- Cholesterol: 0 mg

- Sodium: 70 mg
- Total Carbohydrate: 13.5 g
- Protein: 1.4 g

Quick Asparagus Stirfry

"One of my favorite quick recipes for green asparagus, stir-fried with garlic and olive oil. A squeeze of fresh lemon juice brightens the asparagus up at the end."

Serving: 4 | Prep: 5 m | Cook: 6 m | Ready in: 11 m

Ingredients

- 2 tablespoons olive oil
- 1 clove garlic, minced
- 1 pound asparagus, trimmed and cut into 1 1/2-inch diagonal pieces
- salt
- 1 squeeze lemon juice, or to taste

Direction

- Heat olive oil in a large skillet over medium heat; cook and stir garlic until fragrant, about 30 seconds. Add asparagus and stir-fry until soft but still firm, 5 to 7 minutes. Season with salt and lemon juice.

Nutrition Information

- Calories: 84 calories
- Total Fat: 6.9 g
- Cholesterol: 0 mg
- Sodium: 41 mg
- Total Carbohydrate: 4.8 g
- Protein: 2.5 g

Quick Savory Grilled Peaches

"Grilled peaches are given a slightly savory treatment to make them an excellent summertime side dish."

Serving: 12 | Prep: 10 m | Cook: 5 m | Ready in: 20 m
Ingredients

- 2 tablespoons olive oil
- 1/2 teaspoon chopped fresh basil
- 1/4 teaspoon chopped fresh thyme
- salt and ground black pepper to taste
- 6 fresh peaches, halved and pitted

Direction

- Preheat grill for medium heat and lightly oil the grate.
- Whisk olive oil, basil, thyme, salt, and pepper together in a bowl. Allow flavors to combine for 5 minutes. Brush oil mixture on inside flesh of peach halves.
- Grill peaches, flesh sides down until softened and grill marks appear, about 4 minutes.

Nutrition Information

- Calories: 32 calories
- Total Fat: 2.3 g
- Cholesterol: 0 mg
- Sodium: 2 mg

- Total Carbohydrate: 3 g
- Protein: 0 g

Quick Zucchini Side Dish With Toasted Almonds

"Try this quick zucchini side dish that is literally ready in 15 minutes. The combination of zucchini and slivered almonds is perfection."

Serving: 4 | Prep: 5 m | Cook: 10 m | Ready in: 15 m

Ingredients

- 2 tablespoons olive oil
- 2 tablespoons slivered almonds
- 3 zucchini, cut into short strips
- salt and freshly ground black pepper to taste

Direction

- Heat olive oil in a pan and add almonds. Cook and stir until almonds start to brown slightly, 1 to 2 minutes. Add zucchini and toss with olive oil and almonds. Cook briefly until zucchini are tender, about 5 minutes. Season with salt and pepper.

Nutrition Information

- Calories: 94 calories
- Total Fat: 8.6 g
- Cholesterol: 0 mg
- Sodium: 48 mg
- Total Carbohydrate: 3.6 g
- Protein: 1.8 g

Raisin Plantains

"A very simple and quick way to cook plantain. The great taste and texture of the plantain is complemented well by the raisins."

Serving: 6 | Prep: 10 m | Cook: 10 m | Ready in: 20 m
Ingredients

- 2 teaspoons vegetable oil, or as needed
- 1/2 cup chopped onion
- 3 large green plantains, peeled and grated
- 3/4 cup raisins
- 1/2 teaspoon salt, or more to taste

Direction

- Heat oil in a large frying pan over medium heat; cook and stir onion in the hot oil until slightly softened, 1 to 2 minutes. Add plantains; cook, stirring occasionally, until plantains are crisp and lightly browned, 5 to 7 minutes. The plantain has a tendency to stick together, so the more you stir the more the individual pieces will separate.
- Fold raisins into plantain mixture and cook until raisins are plump and heated, 1 to 2 minutes. Season with salt.

Nutrition Information

- Calories: 248 calories
- Total Fat: 2.1 g

- Cholesterol: 0 mg
- Sodium: 202 mg
- Total Carbohydrate: 61.4 g
- Protein: 2.6 g

Ramp Potatoes

"In the springtime, I always look forward to making ramp potatoes. If you've never had a ramp, you are missing out! A member of the leek family, they have a taste like garlic, onion, and a little something special!"

Serving: 4 | Prep: 15 m | Cook: 30 m | Ready in: 45 m
Ingredients

- 5 large potatoes, peeled and sliced
- 2 tablespoons bacon drippings
- 6 ramps, thinly sliced
- 5 slices cooked bacon, chopped
- salt and ground black pepper to taste

Direction

- Place potatoes into a large pot and cover with salted water; bring to a boil. Reduce heat to medium-low and simmer until beginning to soften, about 10 minutes; drain.
- Heat bacon drippings in a large skillet over medium-high heat; cook and stir potatoes in the hot drippings until golden brown, about 15 minutes. Stir ramps and bacon with the potatoes; season with salt and black pepper. Continue cooking until the ramps are soft, about 5 minutes.

Nutrition Information

- Calories: 567 calories

- Total Fat: 12.6 g
- Cholesterol: 19 mg
- Sodium: 319 mg
- Total Carbohydrate: 102.6 g
- Protein: 14 g

Really Simple Rice

"This is a very simple but tasty rice recipe. Makes a great side dish and leftovers are almost as good the next day."

Serving: 6 | Prep: 10 m | Cook: 25 m | Ready in: 40 m
Ingredients

- 1 tablespoon olive oil
- 1 cup long-grain white rice
- 1/2 small onion, finely diced
- 2 cups low-sodium chicken broth
- 1 pinch garlic salt, or to taste

Direction

- Heat olive oil in a non-stick saucepan over medium-high heat nearly to smoking. Cook and stir rice in the hot oil quickly to toast the rice, 2 to 3 minutes. Stir the onion into the rice; cook and stir 1 minute more. Pour chicken broth over the rice mixture, season with garlic salt, and bring to a boil; reduce heat to low, place a cover on the saucepan, and cook until the broth is absorbed and the rice is tender, about 20 minutes. Remove from heat and allow to rest 5 minutes before lifting the lid.

Nutrition Information

- Calories: 149 calories
- Total Fat: 2.6 g
- Cholesterol: 1 mg
- Sodium: 94 mg
- Total Carbohydrate: 26.9 g
- Protein: 3.6 g

Roasted Asparagus With Herb Goat Cheese

"Roasting veggies always needs revamping every now and then, and I like to experiment by pairing them with different dressings or cheeses. I happened to love goat cheese and had extra on hand. I paired it with asparagus, and they lived happily ever after."

Serving: 4 | Prep: 10 m | Cook: 10 m | Ready in: 20 m

Ingredients

- 1 bunch fresh asparagus, trimmed
- 1 tablespoon olive oil
- salt and ground black pepper to taste
- 1/4 cup herbed goat cheese, crumbled

Direction

- Preheat oven to 400 degrees F (200 degrees C). Line a baking sheet with aluminum foil.
- Arrange asparagus, side-by-side, on a baking sheet. Drizzle olive oil over asparagus; season with salt and pepper. Crumble goat cheese over asparagus.
- Roast in the preheated oven until cheese is slightly melted and asparagus are tender yet firm to the bite, about 10 minutes.

Nutrition Information

- Calories: 104 calories
- Total Fat: 7.7 g
- Cholesterol: 11 mg
- Sodium: 75 mg
- Total Carbohydrate: 4.8 g
- Protein: 5.6 g

Roasted Buffalo Brussels Sprouts

"Highly addictive side dish. The trick to an excellent batch is getting the right level of crispy without burning the sprouts, which requires some attention since Brussels sprouts differ so greatly in size."

Serving: 4 | Prep: 10 m | Cook: 22 m | Ready in: 32 m
Ingredients

- 1 pound Brussels sprouts, trimmed and halved
- 1 tablespoon olive oil
- salt and ground black pepper to taste

- 3 tablespoons butter
- 3 tablespoons hot sauce (such as Frank's RedHot ®)

Direction

- Preheat oven to 400 degrees F (200 degrees C). Line a baking sheet with aluminum foil.
- Combine Brussels sprouts, olive oil, salt, and pepper in a bowl; mix until evenly coated. Spread sprouts onto the prepared baking sheet.
- Bake in the preheated oven until edges are starting to wilt, about 20 minutes. Transfer sprouts to a bowl.
- Heat butter and hot sauce in a saucepan over low heat until melted and smooth, 2 to 3 minutes. Pour mixture over sprouts and stir until coated.

Nutrition Information

- Calories: 156 calories
- Total Fat: 12.4 g
- Cholesterol: 23 mg
- Sodium: 406 mg
- Total Carbohydrate: 10.4 g
- Protein: 4 g

Roasted Butternut Squash Puree

"This is very easy and healthy. It tastes like pumpkin pie!"

Serving: 4 | Prep: 15 m | Cook: 45 m | Ready in: 1 h

Ingredients

- 1 large butternut squash, halved and seeded
- salt and ground black pepper to taste
- 2 cups chicken stock

Direction

- Preheat oven to 400 degrees F (200 degrees C). Place squash on a baking sheet, flesh-side up.
- Roast in the preheated oven until tender and slightly brown, 45 minutes to 1 hour. Cool until easily handled.
- Scoop flesh into a food processor; pulse until smooth. Add chicken stock, 1/4 cup at a time, while continuing to pulse, until smooth. Season puree with salt and pepper.

Nutrition Information

- Calories: 159 calories
- Total Fat: 0.6 g
- Cholesterol: < 1 mg
- Sodium: 395 mg
- Total Carbohydrate: 40.3 g
- Protein: 3.7 g

www.ingramcontent.com/pod-product-compliance
Lightning Source LLC
Chambersburg PA
CBHW071438070526
44578CB00001B/131